Sincerely,

A Conversation to Find Yourself

POONUM DESAI

I humbly offer this book at His feet.

To my mother, father, and the sweetest little noodle,
I love you very much.
Thank you for your endless support, unyielding faith in
me, and memorable laughs.

AUTHOR'S NOTE

My beloved reader, I would first like to express my gratitude. I am grateful you have honored me by reading my words. When I started my writing journey, my laptop was filled with pages of rambling words and broken sentences. My hands could barely keep up with the thoughts racing in my brain. I felt lost in my ideas, dreams, and observations as I navigated the beginning of my life as an adult without the safety net that school provided. I don't think I ever had any intention of turning this into a shared written word, but I figured I can't be the only one who feels that even though life doesn't come with a manual, there is no reason ideas and philosophies can't be discovered. After all, life is a shared experience, and the topics discussed in this book are experienced by everyone, just through different moments. Moments that lead to different perspectives. Perspectives that should be shared and celebrated.

My hope is that on this journey you learn a little bit about yourself and seek to learn from others too, however the channel of that communication may be. While there is room for writing in this journal, you may want to bring your favorite journal along as you read so you can have all the room to be as creative and expressive as you wish. For the chapters that prompt artistry, feel free to look up photos or express your creativity however is best for you.

Good luck on your journey.

CONTENTS

PROLOGUE

O h, Earth. The largest park to ever exist, or at least from what I've seen. A place scented by the intoxicating perfumes of vitality. Tinted with so much color. Symphonies of laughter, hope, dreams, love, tears. The muses of life here are of language, song, nature, art. This planet Earth has much hustle and bustle, the caw of the crow, the thunderous rage of monsoon season, the dying of the leaves marking the season to come, and, of course, the varied actions of the billions of creatures called humans.

I have a pretty busy schedule, but I always make time for a quick break to just enjoy this park. I grab a seat on a different bench every day; I am a bit of an adventurer, you see. I never like seeing the same part of the park twice unless it's been renovated, or if I am feeling nostalgic. Plus, it allows me to hear different stories every day. When you have been around as long as I have, new stories become the most exciting part of the day. It is in these stories I get to see what others say about me and my existence. I believe this activity of observing and listening is called "people-watching."

I like people; they have the most riveting of stories, sometimes a little more dramatic than needed, or absurd, but riveting, nonetheless. Of course, oblivious to my invisible yet omnipresent presence, people feel comfortable enough to say some interesting things about me. Interesting in both the good and bad definitions of the word. But don't worry, everyone is always gossiping about me: some pleased, some angry or sad, some annoyed. I've gotten used to being the subject of talk. I mean, I have no control over what is said; people will believe and act in their own accord.

I will probably forever remain a mystery. Many of you will wonder why I was ever given to you. Some may desire for me to never end, after all, as the famous saying goes, "we fear what we don't know". Many will wonder my intentions. Many are mad at me for coming without a manual.

I argue that is part of my charm. I am not some machine you operate. That would be like asking for a manual on the exact happenings of the universe. You have theories. You have observations. You have ideas. There will never be complete guarantee in the correctness of your findings and conclusions.

How I came to be is up for interpretation, I suppose, but I do not heed too much attention to such a wonder. As long as I am here, I want to focus my thoughts and observations of this park on things that are, things that were, and some things that have not yet come to pass.

At the end of the day, I think most of your species, the species of humans that is, come to similar realizations. As you have more experiences with me, eventually the question shifts from how I came to be, to what I entail. After all, isn't that the repeated question throughout your species' existence? What is the purpose of me?

While the answer to that question involves a rather long quest, I will tell you what I am. I am a third-party viewer, but a fairly involved, intertwined viewer. I study the human experience tediously because humans are complex. And as I sit on my varied benches, I reach my own questions and conclusions spurred from the humans I have so carefully studied. I think it is my own form of meditation. Ironically for me, developing my personal philosophies requires looking within others' reflections, human or not. But like I said, humans require more thought and analysis.

I've heard many times from others that I can be difficult. I won't apologize for my difficulty because my existence is already a lie, for our time together is a brief interlude. Not that your experiences of me are a lie, but a lie because I am but a dream in your journey through this universe. Eventually, I cease. But for the time you and I spend together, I am your truth. My greatest truth is I am not one singular truth. And the discovery of truths can sometimes be ugly. It is a fact that I cannot possibly bloom all the time. Nothing does.

Some of you think that if you play by the rules, you will be guaranteed a safe success. Rather, a safe way to survive. But the problem is, I really don't live by a lot of rules. I am an enigma. And the frustrating thing about me is that there is no one solution to fit all. Believe me, I have seen way too many failed attempts. Every problem, carefully crafted, has a carefully crafted solution to be discovered. Of course, there is always the guidance from others who have had similar problems with me. But this is by no means to be a manual in how to deal with me. This is what I simply wish to convey to you via reflection, analysis, and wonder. This is what I want you to know. What I *need* you to know. All I ask is for your consideration. And when you are ready, maybe some of what I have to say will one day mean something to you.

I think people like to focus on my bad qualities because it is fun to blame someone. But I belong to you—only you can change what you want about me. To look for someone else to fix your problems is a waste of time, for the weeds of toxicity are self-grown, thus self-removed. The ideas in this journal are universally experienced. Only the ideas. My suggestion is to apply these ideas as you see fit.

My existence is your destiny.

My existence is your dreams.

My existence lives within your existence.

My name is Life.

And these are my open letters to you.

PART I

NAME AND SOUL
An Open Letter about Individuality

THE UNSTANDARDIZED STANDARD
An Open Letter about Beauty

ATHENA'S PET
An Open Letter about Education, Knowledge, and Learning

Name and Soul

An Open Letter about Individuality

Individuality

Day 1: The Introduction of Soul

Soul:
an intangible entity
that determines how alive
you feel
beyond the actions of breathing,
eating,
talking,
the basics of living.
Does the soul exist?
Does it go into other bodies when our own body decays?
Does it linger?

Individuality is perhaps my favorite thing about humans. Humans share so many similarities that the desire to distinguish your presence is what makes mankind so enthralling. I think, deep down, everyone wants to stand out. You are not just another employee, another student, another customer. You are a person. You are an experience. You are an individual. A spellbinding creation that no one else can replicate. Ah, but there in lies the question: How can one be unique if there are billions of other creations that are similar?

The trick lies not in being different than the others. It is in being yourself.

Being yourself. No one ever elaborates on the meaning behind that universal slogan. Being yourself is demonstrating unwavering strength in your morals, your beliefs, and your evolution through your experiences. All this without justifying your existence to others, without the approval of others, or without altering who you are in the name of others' acceptance.

Your individualism lies in both your soul and name. Your soul is your voice, and your voice is your name.

Your soul's existence is determined by whether you are living or *living*.

Your name is the one word capturing your irreplaceable heart.

Soul Food

Have you ever thought about your soul and its voice? What does your soul say to you? What do you wish people could hear your soul say?

Checklist:

- Write ten qualities about yourself that you value.
- Write ten qualities about yourself that you would like to improve on.
- Sit in a quiet area for fifteen minutes and breathe deeply for three counts in and three counts out. Write down a situation when you displayed a quality you value, and take a moment to notice your body language when reflecting on that memory. Write down a situation when you displayed a quality you dislike, and take a moment to notice your body language when reflecting on that memory. Are you tense? Did your shoulders rise to your ears? Are you clenching your teeth or gripping your tongue? Take a deep breath. If that situation were to arise again, what might you do differently now, upon further reflection?

Repetition is key to retention. Write your personal mantra that you believe reflects your soul's essence. You will repeat this mantra throughout the discussion of individuality.

Personal Mantra:

Research your name. What does your name mean? Write what you find.

Individuality

Day 2: The Perils of a Silent Soul

The Fields of Asphodel
hosts the most departed souls
in ancient Greece's
attempt to understand Death's realm.
Life lived in a ritualistic manner.
You weren't good or bad,
evil or pure.
You simply were,
simply existed.
In this afterlife,
after the rotations of judgment,
to become a blade of grass in a never-ending field.
A faceless smoke.
An eternally lost soul.

W hile I cannot tell you if the Greek interpretation of Death is correct, I do agree with their emphasis of using your voice. I was given to you to be anything but a faceless smoke. There is no reason your spirit should crumble and decay as the physical body does.

Your soul is the only part of you that has the potential to be omnipresent and survive even once you and I have concluded our time together—at least in the physical sense. If your goal is to leave a legacy, that will require your voice to be present even if your physical essence is not. If you never used your voice, how can your name find its soul? How can you put your name on everything you wanted to possess except yourself? To be different is to have used your voice and remained memorable. True, you have more to risk when you get judged by the good or bad you did.

However, I always thought Elysium was a worthy goal.

Soul Food

What aid can your soul provide in the goals you wish to accomplish from this life?

Checklist:

- Reflect on a time when you kept your essence quiet for the sake of others (whether it be their disapproval, judgment, a desire to make a "good" first impression, anxiety, and so on).
- Write when you feel your soul's voice is most strong. Is it with friends? Family? In a creative outlet?
- Write when you feel your soul's voice is most hindered. Is it with friends? Family? Colleagues?

Personal Mantra:

Thank an individual who encourages you in keeping your soul's voice strong. What would you say to this person to show how grateful you are?

_____

_____

_____

_____

_____

_____

_____

_____

_____

_____

_____

_____

_____

_____

_____

Individuality

Day 3: Uniqueness' Paradox

To follow others' paths
leaves you forever alone,
lost,
uncomfortable.
You do not belong there.
You belong on your path.
Your path is what you have chosen
to reflect your name,
your voice,
your soul,
irrespective of the outsiders.
Uniqueness means to deviate from the norm.
And often the norm,
while comfortable,
can be wrong as well.

How can I tell you how to be "individualistic" when the very term means to be varied from individual to individual? I am universal in the sense that my presence is in all that is alive. But the reception of my presence itself is unique to you. And here lies individuality in all its definition: to be rare is to be irreplaceable. No one can take your slot, and you cannot take anyone else's slot.

In the common interpretation of individuality, there is this misconception that to be unique, you cannot be uniform. My problem does not lie with the idea of uniformity, either. After all, without at least a little uniform, this massive park that is the world becomes difficult to maintain in functionality. Uniqueness' paradox is that unique and normal both share opportunity and obstacle in their definitions. The definitions that are of influence are dependent on the interpreter.

There is opportunity in behaving like everyone else. You will be considered normal, acceptable, and enjoyable to be around. There will be much familiarity and comfort. There is opportunity in being unique, being yourself on your own terms. Much of life will be set by the parameters you choose. The irony of this paradox is the shared obstacle of loneliness.

The obstacle of normal is never knowing the freedom of not serving as a clone, the loneliness in not knowing who you truly are.

The obstacle of uniqueness is the loneliness that will result, because often being yourself entails rejecting the many ideas and habits cultivated by others who are "normal." You will always be an alien to someone who cannot understand the comfort in lying in one's skin without the consistent worry of others' perceptions.

Ergo, you will be an alien to many. But I am not sure if that is truly a problem. After all, doesn't everyone want to know what aliens' superpowers are like?

Maybe it was never telekinesis, but rather, uniqueness.

Soul Food

Which obstacle and which opportunity appeal to you?

Checklist:

- Write five traits about you that make you unique.
- Ask three trusted people to write five traits about you that they think make you unique.
- Compare and contrast your list to the other lists. What do you notice about the way you feel when you look at these lists? Do the qualities make you happy? Sad? Do you focus on a trait because you feel that trait reflects the best version of you? Do you focus on a trait that you are not particularly happy to see on someone's list?

Personal Mantra:

Pretend you're getting a tattoo to showcase your uniqueness. Draw it below.

Individuality

Day 4: The Strongest Drumbeat

*You can only be valuable
by approval
sought from everyone
except yourself.
You are only beautiful
if others verify this truth
without stopping to question
your personal definition of beautiful.
You are only intelligent
if a system confirms this fact
with complete disregard
to your own intelligence.
You only feel validated
if you go through your experience of me
in the same manner as the others,
because then it means you are doing it
"right."
A lie from a poisonous plant that so endlessly feeds you.*

I have observed those who march to beat of their own drum seem the happiest. I think they are happier because they have concluded a similar realization that I know to be truth. Individuality can allow for the building of friendships, love for others, and formation of relationships when there is an open mind to the parameters of *living*. This societal cultivation of lifestyle systemization—often ingrained from youth—is so perplexing to me. I am comprised of millions of pathways, and yet there is only one desirable road worth traveling on?

This whole idea of "right way to live" has dulled the excitement of finding what makes you, individually, come alive. You are a person, not a checklist. Even then, there seems to be only one checklist that is acceptable. There is nothing wrong with wanting what is "normal"—house, marriage, love, wealth, status—but be definable. It's not as if once you have checked the boxes, only then will your life be fulfilled and you will mean something. Checklists are not the ones with an identity.

You have the identity, and you should comprise your own checklist. Let your name become the adjective used to describe your character. Be more than a nice, fun, cool person. Embrace your uniqueness so fully that the only word that can truly describe you is your name. Hopefully, your beliefs, personality, joys, and sorrows lie in your signature. Names have power. Its just up to you to harness such a gift.

Soul Food

What does your drumbeat sound like?

Checklist:

- What are some things you are told to desire, but you are unsure if you truly care for such desires? Write them down.
- What are some things you desire but others told you such desires were foolish or unreasonable? Write them down.
- What sounds reflect your ideal drumbeat? Is it the laughter of your children or loved ones? The cheering of your walking down the red carpet? Your voice when singing to fans?

Personal Mantra:

Find your sanctuary. Where do you feel most at peace where your drumbeat can march without judgment? Consider this: How can you find opportunities to spend more time there?

Individuality

Day 5: Be *Alive*

Your key,
your individuality,
only fits one lock.
This lock can be found
only within yourself.
Your journey is to find that lock.
If your key doesn't work,
cannot effortlessly open a lock,
then it is the wrong lock.
Why we can't have both?
Can there be unique locks opened with multiple keys?
Can there be unique keys that open multiple locks?
An oxymoron of a situation.
Because being unique cannot be imitated.

And so, here we reach the conclusion of discovering your name and your soul.

Your soul and name are your résumé for who you are. I will never understand why more effort is put into a job résumé rather than your personal résumé. And since not everyone will be pleased with your personal résumé, the only contentment that matters is yours. To let others predetermine destiny for you is a debilitating limitation. Other people's valuation system often clouds your true worth because you are using someone else's validation system instead of your own. Your assets may be different than what they find valuable. Your pursuit of life is to discover your true purpose. Your true value. Your name and soul aid in this search. The more authentic and individual you remain, the clearer your destiny and your life become. Whether you believe in destiny or not, I've noticed everything has a funny way of working out just the way it was supposed to. Every time you think you have a grasp on what's happening, I have a curious way of directing you down a path that is meant to teach you a little bit more. And every time you learn a little bit more about yourself, you become a little more alive.

To be *alive* is to embody your name and your soul. To be alive is to have a name and a soul.

Soul Food

Are you alive or *alive*? Are you moving through the motions, or do you feel with purpose, meaning, and vitality in all you do?

Checklist:

- Name three strengths on your personal résumé.
- Name three weaknesses on your personal résumé.
- What is your soul's elevator pitch? Practice this pitch once a week.

Personal Mantra:

Write your résumé—the one that matters. What have your experiences so far taught you? What skills have you developed as a result of situations you have faced? What services for others have you participated in?

_____

_____

_____

_____

_____

_____

_____

_____

_____

_____

_____

_____

_____

_____

_____

The Unstandardized Standard

An Open Letter about Beauty

Day 6: Beauty's Heritage

She had always been told she was beautiful for a woman of her color.
A conditional beautiful.
Her particular color was not known for beauty
but rather for intelligence.
It was impressive that she had any beauty to be appreciated at all.

The mirror, at least in my mind, is the cruelest of inventions. I suppose the mirror is merely a tool. It is beauty, or the idea of its perfection, where the maliciousness of the mirror lies. Reflections are such a troublesome insecurity for all. There are so many "if only" moments—a berating of wishes—to achieve this illusion of faultlessness. How I wish I could cup this woman's face in my hands and wipe her doubt. Her distaste for her shade is amiss. For every color is so much more than a shade. It holds a whole ancestry.

Her name means full moon in a rather romantic and beautiful language known as Hindi, a language from the land of India. India is full of flavorful and spicy food, singers with passionate lyrics accompanied by dance and music worthy of the gods, and clothing so bright and intricate all those who wear it can't help but feel like royalty. Such vivid imagery can be found in any ancestry. Such blindness for such heritage is disheartening. But such is the result when standards of societal beauty are so omitting.

Beauty Marks

Question: What heritage lies in your body and face? What do you know about your heritage? What do you wish you knew?

Checklist:

- Speak with one of your family members. Ask about your heritage and culture.
- Ask a friend or even a stranger about their heritage and culture.
- What is a part of your beauty that you love which is also a part of your heritage?

Repetition is key to retention. Write your personal mantra that you believe reflects your beauty's essence. You will repeat this mantra throughout the discussion of beauty.

Personal Mantra:

Draw five things that are unique to your heritage. Color them with hues you feel represent your ancestry.

Beauty

Day 7: The Cliché of the Dichotomy

Beauty is a Gemini.
And not that beauty is two-faced,
but rather that beauty has split personalities.
There is depth in beauty's shallowness, and shallowness in beauty's depth.
The shallowness in the depth of beauty
forgets the strongest example of subjective perception.
"Beauty is in the eye of the beholder."

Though an accepted universal truth, I've noticed this cliché is believed only provisionally. You—humans that is—deem your beauty valuable only when you have experienced a *rejection* of your brand of beautiful. But until such rejection, it appears there is always some improvement needed. Everyone seems to want what they do not have, especially when the subjectivity of beauty is often disregarded. But I fear the human race has forgotten that comparing types of beauty is oxymoronic.

While the full moon is beautiful to some, with its illuminating glow providing a light in the darkness, it is bothersome to others because it interferes with the darkness allowing peaceful slumber. How can there be this competition of beauty in which only one standard of beauty wins the crown? I think the lenses with which mankind scrutinizes beauty changes the most. More than wealth, fame, happiness, even love. It would be foolish of me to say that the environment you are in doesn't play a role in the way you look at your physical reflection, but to what degree? There are days when society will think you're gorgeous. And there will be days when society will think you need to change parts of yourself to be gorgeous.

Can you possibly keep up with such tumultuous expectations? But if you are your own kind of gorgeous, when you look in the mirror, all you will see is beauty. And if that's all you see, how could you be anything but beautiful?

Beauty Marks

What is your ideal vision of beauty? Think of someone you find beautiful. What about them captivates you?

Checklist:

- Write down a time when you felt stunning.
- Write down three things you have said you would instantly change about yourself if you could. Consider: Where did those desires come from?
- Write three physical traits you love about yourself that you would *not* change for anything in the world.

Personal Mantra:

Study your reflection. What do you see? Ideally, it's best to ask a stranger, but you can ask a loved one to write down what they see when they look at you. Ask them to fold it up. Do not open the piece of paper until you are having doubts about your beauty.

Beauty

Day 8: The Reality of the Dichotomy

One standard of beauty unchanged:
the matter of the unseen beauty, beauty's deeper side.
Thus lies depth of beauty's shallow philosophy.
The beauty of the heart and character.
Illusions of breathtaking beauty fade
as ugliness is to be revealed inside.
Beauty's mesmerizing power,
purity of a kind soul and heart illuminating others' lives.
It seems
no matter the individual, the universal conclusion of beauty:
"Beauty starts on the inside."

I always found it humorous that the discussion of beauty revolved mostly around the women of this world. I have observed the beauty of character seems to be true regardless of any kind of label. For while physical beauty can be appreciated and admired, it fades. Even if it doesn't fade, beauty's radiance cannot be amplified without a heart to match. A genuine smile has mesmerizing power, laughter is contagious, and golden character is hypnotic. The matter of character—the way you make others feel about themselves—is permanent and memorable. For to be beautiful, one cannot stop with the desire to simply be appealing for the eyes only. That is mostly attraction. Beauty is to be appealing of the mind, body, and soul for yourself and for others. Only then have you mastered the art of beauty and attraction. Once you have mastered this art for yourself, you will attract similar beauties. Things you find truly beautiful about others are generally things you should desire to emulate within yourself, for that is where you, personally, find beauty. But finding that true beauty is tricky.

Christmas lights are a lovely experience for many. But what is it about the Christmas lights that are so beautiful? Is it the elation you experience when you see the color against the dark canvas of night? Is it the joy of the lights symbolizing the time in the year when you get to be surrounded by loved ones? When you can pinpoint the source of your awe for the lights' beauty, then you can start to understand what beauty means to you. Only then can you truly understand beauty's depth in all its context.

Beauty Marks

Do you like Christmas lights? How do you feel when you're around them?

Checklist:

- Write three experiences that were beautiful to you.
- Write the names of three people in your life whose inner beauty radiates through and into their outer beauty.
- Smile at everyone you meet today. Give them a genuine compliment.

Personal Mantra:

Draw a heart below. In the heart, write qualities, experiences, and feelings you find beautiful.

Day 9: The Stigma of the Dichotomy

Shallowness in beauty's depth lies on the surface.
Beauty is cunning and sly,
disguised in superficial standards
to evade developing beauty within.
A mania of hunting approval from others.
A consistent battle of trying to impress others.
An endless quest.
An unquenchable thirst.
A gluttonous hunger.

D o not misunderstand me. Beauty is a form of individuality; to be beautiful is not shallow, and to like that you are beautiful is not shallow. However, to rely on the power of beauty alone to build a life is dangerous. Power can be sturdy but blinding. You can easily begin to confuse beauty with love. Beauty with happiness. Beauty with validation of your worthiness to exist. It will be easy to confuse beauty's purpose with beauty's power. Beauty's purpose is to help you see the beauty in all that encompasses this park we share. Beauty's power, while very influential, can sometimes stray from your purpose. It is then that beauty becomes a threat instead of something to be admired. And *that* is a treacherous line to cross indeed. For once you have crossed it, the possibility of return becomes very difficult to accomplish without a complete overhaul of the way in which you live. It becomes difficult to accept the gifts I've come to bear but are deemed unaesthetic. The scars of motherhood. The wrinkles of time. The graying of hair.

You call this age.

Age is one of hundreds of examples in which beauty's shallowness clouds the depth of the gift bestowed. Age is privilege denied to so many.

Age is something to show. The wrinkles around your eyes display how lucky you've been to have laughed and smiled so much. The forehead creases are reminders of the stress and worry that came from hardships endured and defeated. I share with you the most priceless commodity of Time: a gift, that just like me, you get to decide how to use. Surely there is much more you can be grateful for, other than a look of endless youth.

Beauty Marks

Have you ever clouded beauty's purpose with its power?

Checklist:

- Write three things you are grateful for regarding your beauty's purpose.
- Smile in the mirror. Touch your lips, eyes, hair, and eyebrows. Smile and say, "I love you." Give your body self-love.
- Sit with someone older than you and ask about an experience that made him or her feel beautiful.

Personal Mantra:

Draw yourself as you feel most beautiful. Then write why you feel the most beautiful like this. Is there a smile? Is your attitude and energy kind? Is it because you feel confident?

Beauty

Day 10: The Individual Race to the Individual Mirror

Life is and isn't a competition.
Confidence is to be proud of your preparation and performance,
to smile at the results.
And even when you are the best,
be humble enough to understand
number one isn't forever; there are no exemptions from training.
Many say confidence and humility are a difficult combination.
Combination—no, rather supplements—to unleashing beauty's purpose.
Both are perhaps the most important standards in achieving beauty's
unstandardized standards.

Beauty's influence in your life is only as powerful as you allow it to be. There is nothing wrong with wanting to be pleasing to the eyes. But when you cannot see beauty within yourself, you will use anything as a crutch or dependence to fill that void—to no avail. It will stay full momentarily, until the next event comes that shakes your contentment with the material used to fill that hole. The contentment will come as confidence comes. To truly be beautiful is to be confident.

Confidence comes in the understanding that you are who you are with a deep contentment. Of course, there is humility in comprehending the opportunity of improvement, but the search for such opportunities is your wish. Improvement should not be used to one-up a peer you view as competition. There will always be someone more beautiful, smart, funny, athletic—every positive adjective you can imagine—than you. But the only competition worth winning is the competition you have with yourself. Hopefully, to be a better person today than you were yesterday.

But again, all of this is conjecture. The real challenge is to find beauty's dichotomy relevance in your own life. Many live unaware of beauty's cunning words that convey there is only one kind of beautiful. But beauty's purpose lies in the openness to the infinite combinations of beauty's depths and shallows.

Beauty Marks

Have you found your beauty's dichotomy? Have you found shallowness in your definition of beauty? Have you found depths in your definition of beauty?

Checklist:

- Write three times when you have been shallow in judgment of others' beauty.
- Write three times when your views of beauty changed—for better or for worse.
- Perfect your beauty mantra. Then write it down and put it on your bathroom mirror.

Personal Mantra:

Take this book to a mirror and spend a moment looking at yourself. Write down all the beautiful things you see in the mirror, especially the things you take for granted.

Athena's Pet

An Open Letter about Education, Knowledge, and Learning

Education

Day 11: The Gift of Discrimination

The owl:
a symbol of intelligence and wisdom—Athena's favorite.
Ah, but the symbol and the pet are not of the same.
And Athena's pet is not the owl.
The pet is loyal and invisible, hidden until coaxed.
As such, the pet is loyal not just to Athena
but to all offering residence.

All life, both humans and animals, possess a brain. The difference between the brain bequeathed to humans and the brain given to animals lies within the power to discriminate. Mankind can create and understand concepts of right and wrong. Animals have no such limitations or such dominant attributes, and they act in accordance to what is necessary—and no more. For example, animals may kill, but only enough to survive. Because you have the power of discernment, you can ensure your survival and the extent to which you thrive.

The dangerous part of the gift of discrimination was man creating a society in which there is thriving with no regard to the consequences of actions. Furthermore, man forgot that discrimination was a gift. And because of mankind's forgetfulness, they became careless with Athena's pet. Athena's pet is the *willingness* to learn and be educated from all my offerings. Man, as a whole, became comfortable with the idea of a few deciding the way I should be. And as such, too many became complacent in being told what to do—for it is much easier to follow than to lead. Your brains, the most advanced powerhouse on Earth, were not designed to let others decide how the power of your thinking, intelligence, etc. should be tapped. Ignorance is the biggest asset for the manipulative. Ignorance is the biggest tool in one's arsenal to keep the masses obedient.

Report Card

Have there been times in your life when you forgot about the power of discrimination?

Checklist:

- Write your three favorite subjects in school.
- Write your thoughts about your time in an education system. Were you able to use the power of discrimination to determine your schooling path?
- Write down a teacher who taught you about yourself—it doesn't have to necessarily be a schoolteacher.

Repetition is key to retention. Write your personal mantra that you believe reflects your intellect's essence. You will repeat this mantra throughout the discussion of education.

Personal Mantra:

Reflect on a moment when you felt like a puppet in someone else's master plan. How did that make you feel? What could you do differently if it were to happen again?

Education

Day 12: The Lies

They told her she was not particularly smart.
Her strong work ethic—that is how she would survive her life journey.
Twenty years of existence, the epiphany finally shone.
No definition of education or knowledge exists.
We know nothing; to seek understanding is the wisest of them all.
Life is the ultimate test, and there is no right answer.
Believing there is only way to learn is indeed
the most preposterous limitation to learning.

Y ou may quickly begin to find that perhaps the way you want to live your life is different from the templates given. You may realize the "normal" was meant to create order out of chaos and provide a vague guideline, that keeps questions to a minimum. It was always meant to be merely a guide, not a perfect map carved into stone. If you treat the "normal" templates as an unquestionable rulebook, you end up having more questions than answers. But if you ask too many questions, no one will answer you because truly no one knows. In an attempt to stop your questions, they will respond vaguely, "Everyone does that" or "Everyone goes through that" or "You'll figure it out." The truth of me? My truth for every individual is different—just like fingerprints. And your truth can only be uncovered by *you*. That is why no one knows what I am all about.

Truths are nothing but paradox; it's times like these I am very glad to be a third party instead of a direct party. In my cloaked invisibility, I hear the question "What do I do?" when faced with a situation that is foreign to you. I wish I knew every answer. Unfortunately, I cannot tell you. I genuinely don't know. But what I *can* tell you is that every situation presents an opportunity to learn. The only way to figure out which solution works best, is by engaging in the process of learning.

You are both an educator and a student. It is much easier to teach others; you finished your trials in the topic you are now teaching. But it is much more difficult to be the student, for you are only beginning to endure the trial. It is Athena's pet that aids in the transition from student to teacher.

Report Card

When was a time you felt your truth varied from the truth others seemed to have already laid out for you?

Checklist:

- Write three areas you feel incredibly knowledgeable and educated about. It can be anything (video games, fashion, music, books, food, etc.).
- Write three areas you would like to learn more about.
- Find three different individuals who can teach you more in respect to the areas you would like to learn more about.

Personal Mantra:

Write a letter of thanks to a mentor, teacher, or authority figure who made your intellect feel valuable.

Education

Day 13: The Arrival

The pet knocks,
seeking shelter.
Will you grant such a home?
Do not be content in your endless ignorance.
Add four to five.
Add three to six.
Add one to eight.
Subtract two from eleven.
All get you to nine.

A thena's pet will come knocking at your door any time there is something to be learned. So yes, it knocks a lot. The pet can be a permanent resident, should you allow it. Unfortunately, there will be times you may not want to house the pet, because, while the pet has value to offer, you may deem the pet's lesson as a waste of time. Rather, you may judge the pet's education as irrelevant. This is risky because there are different types of education. Athena's pet recognizes this importance and will come knocking when there is a possibility for any kind of education or wisdom to be imparted. Everyone is smart and everyone is ignorant. The bridge from ignorant to smart is mended with Athena's pet's assistance.

But it has become apparent to me that ignorance is acceptable when it is regarding a subject the human society considers unusable. Just because you don't excel in one type of education doesn't mean you aren't smart. Just because one education system doesn't value your specific smarts doesn't mean your smarts aren't valuable.

People may intentionally or unintentionally try to define your intelligence by their valuation system. However, if you can define intellect and education on your own terms, and discover how you learn best, you will always be enlightened. There are so many types of learning and education to be celebrated. So many answers to be discovered. Do not deprive yourself of seeking those answers just because others lied, intentionally or unintentionally, about your worthiness to find them.

Report Card

Have you experienced a time when you felt your intellect—rather, your smarts—were not valuable or up to par with the standard of societal education?

Checklist:

- Find an individual who understands a subject you have struggled with. Ask them if they will explain the material differently than how you have been taught.
- Teach someone about a subject they struggle with that you are knowledgeable in. Break down the material in a manner that can make sense to them.
- Sit with a loved one and research a topic you both would like to learn more about.

Personal Mantra:

Sit outside for a few minutes. Apply a math, science, or art concept to the functions of nature. The shapes on the sidewalks, the birds flying south for the winter, the colors of the leaves, or the role of nature with human psychology and anatomy. How does your body feel as you observe the intertwining of nature and "school" subjects?

Education

Day 14: The Pet's Classroom

The philosophers: Socrates, Marx, Aristotle.
The scientists: Hawking, Newton, Darwin.
Some see in black and white.
Some see in full color and music.
Some see in numbers and symbols.
All minds share specialized inclination.
Comfort in knowledge is devious.
Enslavement of contentment in acumen,
Caged is the pet.
For everything is intertwined.
Smarts and all.

Your society has called the teaching of skills from one generation to another in an organized manner as "an education system." The precedence that the mass organized education system is the only means of learning is false. They do help in the efficiency and quickness of relaying information that is useful, but only to an extent. Teachers in this system are deemed as the only channels of learning, which is naïve and inaccurate.

The school setting is not for everyone.

The mechanism in which learning is carried out through an education institution is not for everyone. You can learn economics, math, and science by becoming a musician. You can learn history, communication, rhetoric, and speech by becoming a public entertainment personality. You can learn and be educated through so many channels.

Honestly, I anticipated most of your education journey to occur through your numerous experiences of me. I did not come with a predetermined system for education. The truth is most learning occurs *outside* the enclosed setting you call a classroom. You learn by engaging in action. You may be lucky and have an educator who sets a useful foundation for you to perform on the world stage, but the *world* is your classroom. The pet can play in your life only when you extrapolate schooling's intended purpose in all aspects of your experiences of me.

Report Card

What suggestions would you make to improve a traditional learning environment?

Checklist:

- If you were an educator, what subject would you teach? For that subject, what's one major lesson you'd want your students to grasp?
- Find another subject that your lesson plan could be applicable to and highlight the integration of the two subjects.
- Sit with a teacher and ask them what struggles they face and their extent of subjects "appropriate" to teach.

Personal Mantra:

Write your ideal seven-hour school schedule. Ask a trusted colleague to do the same. Compare your schedules.

Education

Day 15: The Ego of Wisdom

Intelligence is studying both depth and breadth.
To be wise
is another category altogether.
How can virtue of
experience and time be explained?
If wisdom is to be attained,
it cannot be attained without courage.
The right path, not the easy one.
Face the music instead of fleeing.

Wisdom is a tricky concept, but wisdom undoubtedly only arises after change. Status quo is never a good look for too long. Change is a learning process, and while initially difficult, the process of adapting becomes easier over time in the face of consistent new changes. When you refuse to adjust, the real failure is in your refusal to accept the new hand that has been dealt. Failure to adjust would be comparable to refusing to learn the alphabet for any language you wish to speak simply because you didn't get it right the first, second, or even fifth time. People who are both wise and intelligent are people who seek out knowledge and adjust accordingly. Once they have sought it out, they develop their own interpretations of said knowledge.

Every decade that goes by, more and more information is acquired. I do not believe people are innately smarter as time goes on, necessarily. I just think they have access to a larger collection of accumulated information that can be utilized for personal use. Your society has built virtual and physical libraries dedicated to the mass accumulation of knowledge. Your brain finds companionship in these vast collections of other minds.

But again, Athena's pet can only guide you to the extent you allow. You will only be as educated as you allow yourself to be. Many will be wary of your desire to learn more. It is often inconvenient for the pride of others to be a resource because you have a vast pool of information. Education is never complete. Those who think they have completed their education are disillusioned. I am constantly evolving, which means you are constantly evolving.

Report Card

When you think of wisdom, who or what do you think of?

Checklist:

- Reflect on a time when you felt you handled a hard situation with courage.
- Go out and do something that scares you. Big or small, it is still courageous.
- For one week, practice ten-minute meditation. Yes, ten minutes, alone with your thoughts. The goal is to eventually empty your mind. There are phone apps and websites that provide guidance for this very task.

Personal Mantra:

If you could see yourself five years ago, what would you tell your younger self? Write that here.

Education

Day 16: Until the Departure

Learn.
Other cultures,
other stories.
Other languages,
other people.
Learn now.
This life is merely a song in the grand scheme of time.
Do not wait or hesitate to learn the lyrics at the song's end,
for then it is too late.
While ignorance is bliss,
the truth is always freedom.

I t is true that too much learning is sometimes difficult. It leads to sadness in the depth of understanding people, their habits, and their psychology. It is saddening how atrocious humans can be. But it doesn't have to be that way. The solution is quite simple. Make a home within your abode for Athena's pet. It is possible to learn more and utilize that knowledge to change the present. In your quest for knowledge, there will be, without a doubt, many obstacles you will face, for learning of life often has consistent growing pains.

There is a very inaccurate cliché that attempts to put a positive spin on unfavorable occurrences: "What doesn't kill you makes you stronger." Sometimes, it can leave you debilitated or in a harder situation than you entered. And you will scream, "I wish this never happened!" But it did. There is nothing you can do to change the past. If you are lucky, your struggle to acclimate yourself to a new situation will impart you the gift of wisdom. Wisdom is the strength to adapt and overcome and survive your new reality.

You will get lost on this journey many times. You may not even know where to begin. But even taking one step is a good place to start. Your actions will always show what you value. This, in what you value, is where you will find knowledge. You will discover the art of learning. And then learning becomes a choice, not a decision made by someone else.

Will you ever become all-knowing? No.

Can you become close to all-knowing? That is contingent on the influence Athena's pet has in your life.

Report Card

When will you choose to grant Athena's pet a home?

Checklist:

- With an open mind, listen to someone you disagree with on a topic, but make sure they have prepared legitimate information to back up their argument.
- Sit in a quiet spot and speak kind words to your mind; seek forgiveness when you were too harsh to yourself when you made a mistake.
- Learn in a different manner. If you normally Google something, read a book about the subject. If you normally read a book, watch a YouTube video. If you normally listen to a podcast, ask someone else to teach you with hands-on learning.

Personal Mantra:

**Write down a subject you will dedicate ten hours to learning this month.
Write all your notes and thoughts and aha moments here.**

PART II
Nurture

THE GATEKEEPERS
An Open Letter about Family

DIMES AND PENNIES
An Open Letter about Friendship

THE FIRST WONDER OF THE WORLD
An Open Letter about Love

The Gatekeepers

An Open Letter about Family

Family

Day 17: The Safe Word

Prestige and power are the
guardians of the hearth.
Protectors from inside and outside threats.
First receivers of friends,
first defenders against foe.
Maintain, sustain, retain the homeland.
Competency
is the difference
between peace and siege.

Gatekeepers undeniably have a tough job. For a time, gatekeepers have both the job of leader and nurturer. Competency is the skill that allows the gatekeeper to maintain balance on this trapeze. I suppose the keyword there is *competent*. There are so many interpretations of the word. Presumably, it is often up to the leader to decide whether the gatekeepers are competent. A leader who is war- and power-hungry will have very different expectations of these guardians than a leader striving for long-lasting peace. A leader who is open to economic trade and expansion will have a more open policy than a risk-adverse leader who relies on homegrown sustenance.

But there is a glitch. For while the gatekeeper ultimately serves the leader, how is it possible not to blur the lines between the two roles when the leader depends on the gatekeeper so much to maintain order? This can leave gatekeepers confused about the extent of their role as a leader and the extent of their role as a protector. After all, the gatekeepers chose to protect and serve, not to dictate and demand.

I suppose the most competent of gatekeepers are the ones who can find a balance between leading and safeguarding. Occasionally, force is required to ensure order. Herein lies the biggest problem. Balancing acts require the utmost patience in avoiding collision of multiple objects to prevent damage. For when collision happens, friction is unavoidable. The gatekeepers, whether they applied for the job or not, have responsibilities, personal ideas, and inner desires that may conflict with what the leader thinks is best. When this clash occurs, there will be tension.

Dinnertime

What makes a competent gatekeeper in your eyes?

Checklist:

- When do you feel skilled at a task? Write it down.
- Next time you're engaging in a conversation, take note of how many times you interrupt someone, and how many times someone interrupts you.
- Hold a Lincoln–Douglas debate with someone you tend to argue with.

Repetition is key to retention. Write your personal mantra that you believe reflects your idea of a gatekeeper's nurture. You will repeat this mantra throughout the discussion of family.

Personal Mantra:

Draw or write the skills and weapons an ideal gatekeeper would need at his or her disposal.

Family

Day 18: Gatekeepers Unveiled

In all the positions of this world,
a gatekeeper is perhaps the most highly sought-out job.
Some easily get the position,
some fill a vacancy to shield against destruction,
and some want the job simply because others have it.
An occasional few get placed in a job they never wanted.
The corrupt hold value as much as the virtuous.
Damaged kingdoms have a role.
Pained kingdoms have a role.
Outcasted kingdoms have a role.

L et me alleviate some confusion you may be feeling. You might be thinking I'm giving gatekeepers much more credit and responsibility than the image of gatekeepers you have grown accustomed to. The gatekeepers I am referring to are the gatekeepers of the human lives that comprise me, Life. Within your kingdom, you start as a resident and then become the leader. The gatekeepers of your kingdom are the people who aid in your protection as a resident while you learn the ropes of what it will take to become an exceptional leader. You refer to these gatekeepers as family, or more specifically, parents. Often, many leaders of their own kingdoms take on the role of gatekeeper for a newborn kingdom—a kingdom encompassed in the form of a new child. The hiring process to become a gatekeeper is often questioned, for it is confusing why so many people have the job when not everyone who holds the position understands the value of such an entrusting position.

You see, the kingdoms, hearths, and homes need protection. Whether the gatekeepers ask for a kingdom or not, any kingdom, which carries my essence, will be built. Unfortunately, I do not get to control if these kingdoms are left defenseless or protected. Fortunately, however, I have found that gatekeepers are, for the most part, the best generals to execute the protection of the millions of new kingdoms entering your world and society.

But I cannot deny there are fraudulent gatekeepers, and they play a role just as much as anyone. And gatekeepers lead based on their frame of reference for leadership. If they had poor leadership when they were a resident, they will be a poor leader. As unfortunate as this type of leadership is, I cannot help but feel that suffering plays a role in people's desires to make this world a better place. It is hard to be empathetic toward pain if you have never walked in painful shoes.

Dinnertime

Who are the gatekeepers in your life? Why do you feel like they are gate-keepers—what behaviors indicate this?

Checklist:

- Ask your gatekeeper about their childhood—when they were a resident of their own kingdom.
- Observe similarities of the way they were led and the way your gatekeeper leads now.
- Ask your gatekeeper what their favorite parts (and not-so-favorite parts) about their gatekeepers were.

Personal Mantra:

Pretend you are a gatekeeper, or if you are a gatekeeper, observe your leadership philosophy. Write down your gatekeeping philosophy. What ideas do you mimic from your gatekeepers? What ideas have you changed in your philosophy in contrast with your gatekeepers?

Family

Day 19: Resource Flow

Family comes from sense and feeling,
and are not necessarily predetermined.
Family holds you. Loves you. Laughs with you. Motivates you. Argues with you.
Family is meant to bring you joy. Happiness. Peace. Acceptance. Accountability.
Feel whole when incomplete. Found when lost. Safe when scared. Fulfilled when empty.
Families are not always made by blood.
Friends. Animals. Virtual peers. Nature.
Any root can grow a family tree.

I deally, a family would provide love, support, protection, kindness, and strength to overcome hurdles. Those assets comprise the basic foundations all successful kingdoms are built on. But the expansion beyond the foundation is heavily influenced by the gatekeeper's experience as a resident in their own kingdom. The gatekeeper's experiences, philosophies, and mistakes will outline their scope of protective practices. If the gatekeepers have suffered in their past, undoubtedly the new kingdoms will be affected, leading to a vicious cycle.

Resources such as gratitude, strength, and compassion can break the cycle. But again, the cycle disruption is contingent on whether the gatekeeper does their job, allowing a flow of these resources into the kingdom. For instance, love is a costly commodity, and not everyone can truly afford to buy love or share love once obtained. Some gatekeepers will allow an abundant flow of love. Others may see love as too expensive and will ration the expression of love to ensure a cherishment of love when presented.

Beneficial resources are contingent to the gatekeeper's interpretation of beneficial. After all, interpretations are dependent on the interpreters. Consequently, some gatekeepers may prevent the entry of needed resources; thus, the vicious cycle continues.

I think you find your sense of family when you feel competency in the performance of the gatekeepers, whomever you feel has taken up that role in your life. Often, it is parents, but not all the time. Along with upholding foundational values, a gatekeeper also protects without the condition of protection exchanged for obedience and acquiescence, under the guise of "we know best".

Dinnertime

What resources do your gatekeepers allow? Why do you think that is?

Checklist:

- Thank a member of your family for their leadership.
- Spend quality time with a family member and enjoy a shared hobby together.
- Vocalize to a trusted family member (if they confirm they have the mental and emotional capacity to handle the conversation) any frustrations you have had this week.

Personal Mantra:

Write down the members of *your* family. Who are people that you consider family even though there may be no blood relation? Give them a hug and thank them for being part of your support system.

Family

Day 20: The Keys to the Gates

The key to gatekeeping is devotion.
Devotion to success.
Devotion to kindness.
Devotion to open-mindedness.
Devotion to the kingdom's happiness, even in the face of disagreement.
Without compromise, neither devotion nor love can endure.
Rigidity and unwillingness is a poor precedent,
for "best" is individually determined.
The gift of life is a bequest.
That creation does not owe you anything for being created.

Humans do not like change. I think that's why families are frustrating. There is this expectation that gatekeepers are supposed to unconditionally love you. But I think any love partakes in conditional unconditionality. Problems arise when there is a clash of conditions, and it seems that this clash is a never-ending battle of compromise. You are not the only kingdom around, nor the only guardians around. The desire to want only the best for the residents under your care is wonderful—to a degree. As residents develop this trust, vulnerability, and dependence on gatekeepers, it becomes shocking, disheartening even, when there is a clash of conditions to an uncompromising point. Conditions deemed necessary for survival by the dweller are refused by the gatekeeper, but such situations are where devotion is imperative, perhaps to a greater magnitude than ever before. Because sometimes the compromise is that there is no comprise. There is only devotion to the resident's happiness. To forget devotion is to have lost the precious keys once so desperately wished for.

I never said you had to stay with the same family your entire journey. You may lose families, add to your existing family, or both. You have the option to let your family know your path to be who you are. You have the option to build your own family on the conditions you hold dear to you. With family, the rate of return can be infinity. But devotion and compromise must be invested.

It is a privilege to be a gatekeeper. Your job is to protect, love, and cherish. When you fail to follow the conditions of family, you have damaged the keys given to you. I can survive without nurture. But I will never thrive.

Dinnertime

If you chose the position of gatekeeper, how will you choose to guard such a gift?

Checklist:

- Write down five lifestyle conditions that are nonnegotiable to you (e.g., life partner, job, gender, sexuality, etc.).
- Pretend you are a gatekeeper. Write down how you would handle a clash (such as gender, job, dreams, etc.) with your resident that, to you, is foreign.
- Reflect on a time when you were a kid and you and your parent or caregiver clashed. Now that you're older, reflect on *why* your parent or caregiver did what they did. How can you apply this lesson to your own (should you wish for them) children one day?

Personal Mantra:

Draw a scene where you feel the happiest with your family. Take time to consider who is there, where you are, and what you are doing.

Dimes and Pennies

An Open Letter about Friendship

Friendship

Day 21: The Coin Collection

There is a land
located in the Northern Hemisphere
called the United States of America.
And in this land, four of their greatest leaders
are imprinted on circular bits of metals called coins.
Metallica: the quarter, the nickel, the dime, and the penny.

A lucky penny here, a lucky quarter there. I always found it odd that coins in general were always seen as low in value, but any time there is a coin on the street, people will rush to pick it up. Perhaps the coins are not as underrated as perceived. Alone, the values of these coins are not much, but combined, their value can amount to a purchase. Not in a great amount to which a house can be bought, but sufficient that if you were to check behind enough cushions, a nice cup of coffee can be bought, courtesy of strangers and their loose change.

Friendships function very much like these coins. The obvious interpretation would be best friends are quarters, close friends are dimes, good acquaintances are nickels, and people you know no more than beyond a first-name basis, are pennies. Ideally, everyone wants a bunch of quarter-value friendships. Quarter friendships don't really have a niche in their friendship because they are reliable in every aspect of your life, an absolute advantage, if you will. But, of course, you can only have so many best friends.

Most people have very few nickel friendships. Nickels aren't worth the effort in maintaining a dime-level friendship; but they require more than a penny-level friendship. As time moves on and your life gets busier, finding that balance simply becomes more work than what you extract from the friendship. Thus, the most common type of friendships are dimes and pennies. All combined, these four are the value of your friendships.

Appraisal Sheet

What is in your coin collection? Quarters, dimes, nickels, pennies?

Checklist:

- Go through your phone contacts. How would you classify each friendship? Go through your social media accounts. Are there some pennies it would be in your best interest to unfollow?
- Identify your quarters.
- Identify your nickels.

Repetition is key to retention. Write your personal mantra that you believe reflects your idea of friendship's nurture. You will repeat this mantra throughout the discussion of friendship.

Personal Mantra:

Draw a quarter, dime, nickel, and penny. Classify every friendship in your life in one of these categories.

Friendship

Day 22: The Collection's Value

With ease can one hundred pennies be found.
More ease than three or four dimes, let alone ten.
A full dollar is an illusion.
The immeasurable treasure of ten dimes is Atlantis,
But quality over quantity lights the way to the lost city.
The light only shows for heroes of quality.
Time explains this preference, the many more pennies than dimes.
Pennies can fill silence quicker,
temporarily alleviate loneliness,
and make the darkness seem lighter.
And the truth is,
sometimes you need that.

There is a very important condition that must be applied so a friendship can be appraised truthfully and accurately.

Reciprocation.

However you categorize a friend does not necessarily determine their value in your life. A friend's value lies in the amount of friendship that can be bought (if it could be monetized). The amount a friendship can buy is based off both sides' valuations combined. If you are lucky, you will have one quarter friendship in your life. Truly beyond blessed to have two. These are friendships that will hopefully last till the end of both your days. This is simply because dedication to quarter-value friendships is high-maintenance. Nickel friendships just don't add enough value to justify the work required to sustain the friendship. That leaves the dimes and the pennies.

So often I hear, "I'd rather have ten dimes over one hundred pennies." Of course—who wouldn't? The question is: Are you giving that same effort in return? The trick to finding more dimes than you anticipated is to be a dime yourself.

But being a dime to everyone is exhausting. Humans were never designed to be alone. Sometimes, you just need a companion to roll with you during the good times and enhance them to become great times. And this is the pennies' sole use. Pennies, for the most part, are not there during the hard times. They politely listen to your complaints and frustrations but will try very quickly to end the uncomfortable conversation and move on to a more pleasant one. This does not mean your pennies are bad people; they simply serve a very specialized function, and to expect anything beyond that would be foolish.

Appraisal Sheet

Who are your pennies? Do they drain you at all?

Checklist:

- Show gratitude to your penny friendships. Express your thanks for their presence.
- Look at your last appraisal sheet. Write down how many pennies you have.
- Reflect on your pool of currency. Are you satisfied with your friendships so far?

Personal Mantra:

Next time you are with your penny friendships, observe how you feel after you hang out. Do you feel happier? Tired? Excited?

Friendship

Day 23: Dime Piece

Dimes are of multifunction use but with a comparative advantage.
May it be spirituality, honesty, or other, the niche holds the value.
In true acceptance, "flaws" and all.
Flaw is an ugly word.
Flaws are yin-yang.
Passion cannot be without anger.
Strength cannot be without the power of no.
Kindness cannot be without excessive empathy.

While they do take a more significant amount of time to develop, dime friendships will be there through the good and bad moments and will befriend most aspects of you. I say *most* because dimes, in contrast to quarters, tend to see traits as flaws instead of part of who you are. While undoubtedly you will have vices, eliminating those vices should occur because *you* realize their toxicity in your life. They bring *your* individual happiness down. Changing those vices for others is not sustainable. Such an action creates this mirage that if you change this part of yourself, then you will be worthy of friendship.

It is very similar to the idea of losing weight with the intention of living a healthy lifestyle in contrast with trying to lose weight so people will find you attractive.

It is much easier to find vices in others than yourself. As friendships get deeper, so does your awareness of your friends' faults. As much as changing vices for others is unsustainable, so is demanding change in others to continue a friendship.

But that being said, if a vice is too much to handle, you can leave the friendship; however, be honest about your departure. Prior to your departure, check yourself too. Sometimes you are the toxic one.

Appraisal Sheet

Who are your dime pieces? Would you want them to evolve into quarters?

Checklist:

- Show gratitude to your dime pieces. Express your thanks for their presence.
- Look at your appraisal sheet from the first activity. Write how many dimes you have.
- Engage in an activity that someone you identify as a dime piece enjoys.

Personal Mantra:

Do you want more dimes in your life? Evaluate actions you could take to create stronger friendships.

Friendship

Day 24: Rust

Honesty is not cheap.
Society isolates the honest.
The truth is rarely enjoyable and pretty.
Truth is an open exchange.
Honesty cannot be given without critiques.
Genuineness cannot be given in the face of jealousy.
Should you carry the burden that is truth,
be warned: it is heavy.

Of the many complaints I hear against me, the lack of genuine and honest friendships is among the top. I think these friendships are so hard to find because there is disparity in the appraisal of the friendship value. Disparity in friendship value arises when the effort becomes one-sided and the friendship gets rusty. Even dimes can rust. You cannot expect dime-quality relationships when the only effort being exchanged is penny quality. And sometimes there are misinterpretations about the level which effort is exchanged. Sometimes you only want to be a penny to someone who values you as a dime, or you value someone as a dime when they only see you as a penny. But for the friendships you crave, both sides must agree about the quality, or you will never know how much that friendship can buy.

Once you have determined what your friendship can buy, it is important that the friendship remains a product worth investing in. If the quality of a friendship deteriorates, that is as much of a concern as the miscommunication of the friendship status. In conjunction with the one-sided dilemma, many friendships fail because the friendship has become draining. This occurs when one party has too many free expectations of the other. But remember, there is no such thing as a free lunch. Everything has a price.

Appraisal Sheet

How many rusted friendships have you been in? Are you in one now?

Checklist:

- Take an audit of your friendship. If you've let the ball drop with a friend, apologize to him or her.
- Thank a friend whom you feel has always been honest with you, regardless of how uncomfortable the conversation.
- Send a meme to a friend to brighten their day.

Personal Mantra:

Reach out to a friend you know who may be struggling right now. Invite them over for a night in to catch up.

Friendship

Day 25: Toxicity and Character

Therapy.
The functions of the occupation
require a strong ear to fears, envies, anxieties.
Compensated for work expected to be free
from a friendship.
The tsunami of emotion is too much.
No matter the strength of capacity,
there is a line even if in sand.
Taking without replenishing.
Talking without listening.
Attention without respect.
Bitterness and toxicity begin to sow
as the one-sidedness grows.

Friends are truly such an underrated support system. Friends are often the people who put you back together. Your character will always exemplify what you wish from a friendship. I've noticed the friendships that last the longest are the ones where both sides found a common ground in morals and values. Religion, race, gender, and sexual orientation become less important or less pertinent to the friendship as the friendship grows deeper.

And it's not as if friends do not fight. But the growth comes in the process of mending the friendship. It's in the growth of friendship that you begin to understand the meaning of companionship. The first step to remedying any kind of poison in a relationship is listening. If you don't allow an open channel of communication between you and your loved ones to work on those problems, none of your relationships will work. Individuals who toss aside your feelings instead of listening are not your friends. Your honesty will make them angry because it highlights their wrongdoing. A mind dedicated to intentionally misunderstanding your intentions is nothing more than a waste of time. Without communication, there cannot be depth. The depth of a friendship is not always linear to time spent in the friendship, so some friendships are nothing more than a test of time.

When it comes to friendships, remember this: Rarely is anything in life a solid dollar amount. There is always some cent amount added.

And when you are lost and digging behind the cushions because you don't have enough money to buy that badly needed cup of joe, coins come to the rescue. Do not forget about the cents in wealth.

Appraisal Sheet

How much are your friendships worth? Be honest.

Checklist:

- Frame a picture of yourself with your friends. They can be of any coin value.
- Befriend one new individual whom you would like to add to your coin collection this week. (Try saying hello to someone you see often but have never interacted with.)
- Send out positive energy for all of your friends today.

Personal Mantra:

Write a letter to a friend of your choice and express your feelings about them.

The First Wonder of the World

An Open Letter about Love

Love

Day 26: Love's Form

A beautiful feat of man meant to honor a legacy, commemorate a death.
A departure so painful to bear,
there was no greater honor than the composition of an architectural masterpiece.
A glorious harmony of multicultural influences in design, art, creativity, and labor.
An ivory-coated colosseum: resting on shimmering marble
whose color changes with the light.
The walls inscribed with onyx ink; the halls' decorated artwork carved from hand.
The archway preceding the mausoleum, a sight fit for gods,
a privilege to the common folk.
Two decades, over twenty thousand laborers,
hands raw with the vigorous work, guided by the light of sun and moon.
An architect's vision of perfection.
Onlookers submerged in appreciation.
Love. All in the name of love.

L ove is perhaps the biggest oxymoron. An enjoyable pain. A way to die while still breathing. A beauty with ugliness. A peaceful illusion in warmongering reality. I think that is why humans seek love so much. Any love, not just romantic. Although, I have postulated, romantic love has a very different kind of reimbursement system than other loves. The payout in the reciprocation of love is so high, that often the risk—regardless of how high the stakes—is brushed aside. But the ridiculously frustrating part of love's risk is that you cannot use logic and analysis to "think through it" as many of you, I am sure, can attest. Love is something that you, a person with a heart but also a brain, have absolutely no control over. That is both invigorating and terrifying. It is hard to do preventative preparation because you cannot prevent love's infiltration. It just happens.

You cannot help whom you fall in love with. Your heart, against the brain's conditions and rationalities, will pick whomever it chooses. Love is a journey that bears both the anticipation and excitement of navigating your path with no map. And that thrill—the thrill of love—is addictive. Due to the dependent nature of love, similar addictions such as lust and obsession can be misidentified as love. Real love is when there is an intertwining of selflessness and gratitude.

You have felt the concept of love since your individual kingdom was born. Be it family, friends, teachers, coaches—you have known how to love and be loved via these individuals. Music, movies, writing, or anything that allows you to express your individuality lets you fall in love with the essence of me, again. While there is pain in all love, it is romantic love (if such a love is of interest to you) that many of you often discover Love's cruelty for the first time. Rather, it is in romantic love you can feel the highest, but in equal consequence, can feel the harshest mellow.

Love Letter

What visuals flash in your mind when you think of love?

Checklist:

- Write what romantic love feels like to you.
- Guess what the wonder of the world is referred to in the beginning poem.
- Ponder the question: What would be an ideal monument to show someone's love for you?

Repetition is key to retention. Write your personal mantra that you believe reflects your idea of love's nurture. You will repeat this mantra throughout the discussion of love.

Personal Mantra:

Draw the monument you imagined from the third point on the checklist.

Love

Day 27: Love's Duality

Romantic love is different.
New loves can be discovered,
but "love is blind" becomes clear.
A heart enamored by another heart,
so desperately desiring their junction.
The heart just chases, and logic takes some time to catch up, if at all.
The shattering of glass is your heart.
The captivating euphoria is now the excruciating withdrawal.
The ecstasy is lost until your heart rises once more.
And sadly, some loves are irreplaceable.

The power of love is immeasurable. I think that is the only reason man chases love over and over again, despite the torturous nature of love's departure. It is in love's unconditional conditionality that its power resides. For to wield a power so strong to create such a sense of selflessness, where your happiness is intertwined with someone else finding their happiness, is an unconditionally giving condition. But in this very reason also lies the explanation to the question "Why can't there be more love in the world?" These unconditional conditions get broken often for various reasons. When love is trying to be repaired, how can love also be given?

The healing from love's bite is long and tedious, for love's infectious happiness is deep. Every single person on this planet comes with conditions. It would be impossible to exist without them. For it is within your conditions that you outline your morals, ethics, acceptances, beliefs, and desires. Conditions are part of defining individual essences. Then suddenly, out of nowhere, there comes this invisible force, crumbling your pillars of conditions to dust. It is not that your conditions themselves left; it is your adherence to these conditions that is now wavering for incomprehensible reasons. Unconditionality lies in the disregard of compatibility between differing conditions' because the two hearts desperately long for each other's presence. In this desire, there is unrestricted dedication to any action necessary to keep the two hearts together, even if they should not be.

Compatibility.

It either severs or strengthens the bond of the unconditional conditionality of love's power.

Love Letter

What does compatibility mean to you?

Checklist:

- Write down a time when you confused initial chemistry as compatibility.
- Write down your conditions for a strong, viable love. This is different than your conditions for attraction.
- Write about a time when you have felt deeply loved. It does not have to be romantic.

Personal Mantra:

Write down a time when you faced a situation that lacked compatibility. How did you overcome this situation? After reflection, is there anything you would do differently?

Love

Day 28: Love's Loophole

Love's wisdom is won in a bet.
It lies in the discernment of sustainable possibility and a highly probable fallout.
The bluff is reciprocation.
Lack of such stems resentment.
Survival is love. Umbrage is poison.
Givers and takers are both greedy,
but one lives and one withers.

Unfortunately, love has a loophole—a detrimental one at that. The loophole, often taken advantage of, is that one can simply change their conditions to match the conditions of the chosen heart, mistaking that transference as unconditional love. That is a dangerous loophole, because there are always negative externalities. In addition, you have shifted your essence to match a mold that you don't quite comfortably fit in. That cannot be sustainable. Eventually, someone gets bitter and angry because they gave up so much of themselves. That is not compromise; quite the opposite, in fact, for compromise is a two-man game. Resentment can begin to breed. Keyword is *can*.

This loophole may serve you well, but more likely, it won't. The truth is there will be many who give more love than they receive. They know love is an essential resource to survival, and when they see someone needing this resource, they will immediately do what they can to fill the gap. If you are one of these people, I warn you to proceed with caution. It is an extremely painful life to always give. You will spend your entire life wondering why no one else reciprocates. The reality of the same reciprocation is minimal. People are deemed as "selfish" for taking so much love, but it is a survival technique.

I am not saying it isn't cruel—wicked, almost—but of course, they will take your help. If you set yourself on fire to keep others warm, that is on you. You choose what you give of yourself. You cannot be angry that you chose to give something under the guise of being unconditional, when in reality you were hoping for the condition of reciprocation. If you choose to give, it must be under the parameters you are comfortable with freely giving. Once you have found the conditions under which you have loved yourself, only then will you find compatibility in the love you seek.

Love Letter

Have you ever taken advantage of love's loophole? How so?

Checklist:

- Write about a time when you gave more love than you received.
- Write about a time when you took more love than you gave.
- If you have never been in love, write down your own observations of love. Do you seek a romantic love? Write why or why not.

Personal Mantra:

Ask five people, maybe friends or on social media, what their definition of love is and write down their responses. Compare their definition to yours.

Day 29: Love's Wound

Love of your life.
Your one true love.
Love until the end of time.
The love to form marriages.
The love every princess dreams of.
The moonshine of love.
Movie love.
Soul-mate love.
Love in the unifying flames of passion and chemistry.
Such a power is fearful and admirable.
For even Death
does not remotely have that type of influence.

It seems apparent that altering conditions does not to yield the long-term feasible results most people desire in love. Yet it happens so often. There will be—if you are lucky or unlucky, that's up for your determination—*the* love. You will never have one quite like it ever again. It will be the "when you know, you just know" kind of love. This love ignites flames within you that you have never felt before. But many times, these are not the people you end up spending the rest of your life with. Not all flames are meant to be joined to create a bigger flame. For while the flames are intense and bright, joining the flames may lead to a deadly fire instead of a brighter illumination. This is often because the conditions, deep down, do not match. Even if the conditions *do* match, the timing of the meeting may be unfavorable. But the most painful possibility is the one-sided ignition of flames. The reasonings are irrelevant, for the outcome is excruciating, often life-changing.

This is the ugly side of love's power: the power to kill. It may not physically kill, but it impales something, disables something. And you are stuck in the past, remembering who you were before your heart was broken. And anyone who tries to love the new you is almost like loving a ghost. A ghost so desperately wishing to live its old life without realizing it is still alive. Subsequently, the cycle of heartbreak endures. Some argue that the beauty of finding "the one" is that you get thrown in the deep end. While you have to struggle to survive, you also experience the deepest depths of love, immersed in water's truest nature. But some argue the struggle wasn't worth it. Not only did they drown, but now they can't appreciate any other body of water because they can think only of the ocean's grandeur despite the ocean killing them.

I don't think there is a right or wrong way to view love. When it comes to love, every creature and person I have observed has a different experience with a different analysis.

Love Letter

What are your thoughts on finding *the* love?

Checklist:

- Reflect: Would you rather journey to the deep end or stay near shore?
- Reflect: Do you think there is recovery from metaphorical drowning?
- Sit near a body of water. Stay here for as long as you like. Imagine yourself swimming through the body of water. How far would you want to go?

Personal Mantra:

You have decided to embark on the journey of love. Prepare your toolkit to help you through this journey. How will you handle the good times and the bad? Do you have a strong support system? Do you have healthy communication methods? Do you have healthy compromise skills? And of course, do you have chocolate?

Love

Day 30: The Small Sea

The best-friend fantasy;
the winning of the lottery.
But it is just that: a lottery.
The ease, the understanding, the lack of struggle.
Eyes for only one, butterflies for only one.
Partner in crime. Ride or Die.
Could this be so?
But such ignorant bliss is ruined.
The loss of not one, but two.
The biggest what-if. The biggest desire.
The lucky ones
are those who fall out
instead of stay in.

Love is a hard topic for anyone to talk about. I know. I see all the lonely occupied benches. I see the fear. I smell the alcohol in the air. I see the leftover foods of comfort in the trash can. All coping mechanisms, I imagine. The tricky part with finding the one is in the rarity of both parties' puzzle pieces being perfect matches for each other. Some argue that if it doesn't match, then it wasn't the true one. I think that is up to your belief and the understanding of the love you experienced. Everyone else's words are simply conjecture. The same cliché is always offered: "There are plenty of fish in the sea." Your ship, however, can only cover a certain amount of the sea, which means you are only exposed to the fish in that area. Additionally, only you can know the value of the fish you caught. And often, the first fish you ever catch will determine how you will choose to fish in the future.

To me, the real reason your first love is memorable is not so much because of the person, but because that was the first time you experienced love's excitement *and* love's deep cut. The person is a vessel through which love flows, but to me, I think, you remember the love more than the person. You understand the protection, the comfort, and the happiness that physical touch can provide. But there is little discussion about the harshness of the strong likelihood that your first love is not the one you end up with. That's why they say it's so lucky if you do. You fear you will never love anyone the same way.

The great thing is that you will fall in love again, just differently than the first time. Often, you find love multiple times via different people, and you will love each romantic experience differently.

Love Letter

What is a conjecture about love that you do not agree with?

Checklist:

- Write one negative coping mechanism you have. Write a positive coping mechanism you could switch the negative one with.
- Have you used a dating app to expand your sea? Write down your experiences.
- What would you tell your five-year younger self about love?

Personal Mantra:

Draw the ideal fish you would like in your sea (should you have such a desire). What characteristics do they have? Where could you meet these fish?

Love

Day 31: The Taj Mahal

The true beauty of love is that there is no one defined road in which this can go.
How can there be a well-traveled road to a destination that often presents itself
when you least expect it?
There is power in learning from others' mistakes.
The mistake of pretending to be in love.
Mistakes in lack of recognition that love can be the cure for some and yet cancer for others.
The flag of surrender for some, and yet others' atomic bomb.
The breath of fresh air for some, and the suffocation for others.
The angel for some, and the devil for others.
And you will be the "some" on days and the "others" on different days.
In the entirety of the oxymoron that is love,
perhaps the most sense that can be made of love
is love's senseless logic,
love's unison among division,
the life love can bring to the lifeless.

L
ove is not always compatible, and compatibility is not always love. But if you want a life partner, perhaps it is in the potential of love's growth that matters more than the love itself.

I've heard people say it's so romantic to love only one person your whole life. I think that is such a lonely way to live. Sometimes, love doesn't grow together or in the same direction. You evolve; therefore, your loves evolve. It's okay not to want to be together forever. Nothing is forever. Do not see letting go of something you have invested so much time in as a waste. It has molded you and shaped you into a new being that is ready for new experiences. Commitment to a love is important, but commitment to a love for the simple sake of commitment is very lonely indeed. Healthy relationships require healthy minds, bodies, and souls; when people are lacking in any, and there is fear surrounding love, love begins to morph into a façade.

The Taj Mahal is, in all of its splendor, first and foremost, a tribute to love. While I have focused mostly on romantic love, love of any kind similarly follows the parameters I have outlined. Love requires nurture to survive. All love is essential to man's survival. Love's real wonder lies within its Pandora's box—like nature. When you open yourself up to love, you release other mirroring potentials. Jealousy, anger, dependency, and sometimes your individuality. But you also open yourself up to happiness, freedom, and bliss. Love can be an open-ended resource. That is why it is the first wonder of the world. But its abundance or scarcity in your life, my friend, will always be dependent on you.

Love Letter

How will you choose to use the first wonder of the world?

Checklist:

- What wonder of the world, such as the Taj Mahal, would you love to visit in your lifetime? Why?
- Create a wonder of the world that best reflects you. It can be a drawing, poem, song, story, or photo, whatever captures your love.
- Spend quality time with your significant other. Ask them how you can be a better partner to them.

Personal Mantra:

Create a vision board or a Pinterest board of your wonder of the world.

PART III

Treasures

INFRASTRUCTURE
An Open Letter about Health

GREED'S INVISIBLE HAND
An Open Letter about Wealth and Money

THE DORMANT LION
An Open Letter about Success and Redefining Yourself

THE MISNOMER
An Open Letter about Dreams

THE CRY OF THE PHOENIX
An Open Letter about Loss and Death

THE MAN-MADE SUNRISE
An Open Letter about Happiness

Infrastructure

An Open Letter about Health

Health

Day 32: Highway to Health

Six Flags over Texas.
Bluebonnets and pecans.
A proud heritage of football and the contraction "y'all".
To connect the vast lands
Highways assembled by man.
Mechanisms easing commerce and transportation.
Susceptible to traffic,
the highway becomes what it swore to destroy:
a deterrent to speed,
fosterer of congestion.

I nfrastructure, while perhaps costly in taxes, is essential to the functionality of any city. As the city's population grows, the need for highways grows so traffic can move quicker. Don't get me wrong. Congestion is unavoidable, and even if you plan accordingly to avoid congestion, it is never a guarantee that you will have a completely clear drive. And often with congestion, the highway is still the only, and fastest, way to your destination. Infrastructure has limits in its operative capacity. Furthermore, just like any machine, it requires consistent maintenance in order to extract maximum use before it becomes unusable.

Your health is your infrastructure. Too often, humans see the body as the only infrastructure, but the body is only one highway in the network of highways that make up your infrastructure. You can only utilize your infrastructure to its maximum capability under two conditions.

The first condition, which is incidentally dependent on the second, is the efficient maneuvering of traffic on every single highway. The second is that the highways are maintained consistently with immediate attention to dangerous problems. Your health is dependent on the integrated well-being of all highways working in unison. For when one highway is suffering, the problems begin to trickle into *all* the other highways. And while this seems like a no-brainer, I have often discovered people will focus on the highways with the best scenery, and in the process, ignore the other highways; as such, they fail to maintain the "less scenic" highways.

While your individual network will be constructed differently and require varied maintenance procedures, there are four universal highways: mental or psychological health, emotional health, physiological health, and spiritual or ethical health.

Results of Physical

Do you tend to neglect a highway in your infrastructure? Which one? Why?

Checklist:

- Find one positive action that would improve a neglected highway in your life.
- Integrate one continued maintenance method for a highway, such as exercising, reading, or painting each day this week.
- For ten minutes every day, meditate and focus on your breathing for five counts in and five counts out.

Repetition is key to retention. Write your personal mantra that you believe reflects the treasure of health. You will repeat this mantra throughout the discussion of health.

Personal Mantra:

Draw the four highways and connect them together. Under each highway, write three maintenance tools you use to support the upkeep of each highway.

Health

Day 33: The Fabulous Four

In truth, it is not so much health itself that seems to be arduous.
It is in the consistency of required maintenance.
It is in the extensively expensive conditions which comprise strong health.
For sturdy highways,
quality labor and materials are to be employed.
Long-term construction time lines are essential for resilience.
For timeliness manages potholes.
The reward is swift arrival and tempered rage.
Subpar foundations are fragile and dangerous.
The cost is frustration and repetition.

Y ou only get one life. You get one body, one brain, one heart, one soul. You may do what you will to extend life as your health begins to deteriorate, but even if you do, you still only have one of each.

Your health is a lifestyle, and your lifestyle is your health. You cannot hope to improve the quality of one without improving the other. The body can do everything: mend, repair, detox, build, bear children. The mind is the most intelligent creation on this planet. As the smartest computer in the world, the brain can theorize, innovate, dream, create both beauty and hideousness, produce both light and dark. The heart can mend gaps; love seems to be the secret solution to any obstacle endured. The soul projects voice the past, present, future, and into the afterlife. It is within your soul you find purpose, establish perspective, and build character.

These feats can only be achieved to the extent in which you invest in your health. Your body will deteriorate if you do not use it or if you nurture it with cheap materials, such as poisonous food and drink with no nutritional value. Your mind will remain stagnant if you don't challenge it, because labor without mind-fullness disregards the depth of the brain's capacity. Your heart cannot grow if you are selective in your love or closed off from receiving love. This goes for platonic love, romantic love, and familial love. Your heart will not be nurtured if you believe there is only one way to love, or if you remain rigid in your demonstration of love. Your soul will never find the place of understanding it so desperately seeks if you cannot find your purpose. Finding purpose requires trial and error, often with a side of disappointment. But it is in that disappointment that your soul finds more clarity and contentment as you increase your understanding of all I entail.

Results of Physical

Is your health in unison? Are you at 100 percent in each category? If not, why do you think that is?

Checklist:

- Call upon Athena's pet. Read a book, watch a video, or Google an activity you can do to improve at least one of the four highways.
- Go to bed early each night this week.
- Spend ten minutes with nature every day for a month.

Personal Mantra:

Draw four pillars and label each one with a health highway. Contemplate on why you might be neglecting improvements to a certain highway. Is it fear? Laziness? A lack of desire? A lack of knowledge?

Health

Day 34: The Bluff of Shortcuts

The biggest gamble of all is to live without this unison of health.
The biggest payout is living with this unison for as long as possible.
But betting is a risky venture,
for high payouts lack guarantee
and require forces beyond feasibility.
Curve balls will be continuously thrown to disrupt the balance.
Consistent construction on the highways, while unpeaceful,
is the road to peace,
for more problems always arise.
Action is hard. Talk is easy.
But take comfort:
Good health is worth the discipline.

*W*hen it comes to health, there are no shortcuts.

The endless search for a shortcut will forever be futile because your health is dependent on regular nurture. There is no pill that will cure weight gain or acne, because as your body changes, so will its needs. There is no one book that will give you all the knowledge of the world, for knowledge cannot be contained in a single book. There is no perfect love in which you are always happy, because love is about compromise, two entities attempting to act harmoniously. There is no easy way to discover your purpose, because finding your purpose requires an unearthing for a passion, which can take years. This is a cyclical and consistent process that you must maintain.

When there is an upset in the homeostasis, you must employ even more resources to remedy the pothole. There will be both permanent and temporary upsets in all four health categories. Your body can have permanent disruptions, such as asthma, or temporary disruptions, such as occasional back pain. Your mind can have permanent disruptions, such as ADHD, or temporary disruptions, such as depression and anxiety—and sometimes even those are permanent. Your heart can have permanent disruptions, such as removing a destructive individual from your life, or temporary disruptions, such as over-coming an uncomfortable confrontation with an individual you value in your life. Your soul can have permanent disruptions, such as when the embers of passion can no longer be ignited, or temporary disruptions, such as a sabbatical from exploration and adventure.

It is your job to remedy the temporary potholes and maintain your infra-structure despite the permanent potholes. If you decide to do nothing, your health level will reflect so.

Your job is to find which methods work best to achieve your desired health status.

Results of Physical

How will you build your infrastructure? What is one change you can make for each highway to better their structure?

Checklist:

- Write some permanent upsets to your health homeostasis.
- Write some temporary upsets to your health homeostasis.
- Write a time you indulged a shortcut. Write your experience about your success with the shortcut.

Personal Mantra:

Find the best answer for you. Create two columns, one labeled temporary upsets and the other labeled long-term upsets. In each column, write solutions that have worked for you in the past to deal with your problems. Rate each solution on the sustainability of the solution.

1 = unsustainable for more than a short period
2 = moderately sustainable, but still not ideal solution
3 = sustainable and aids in continued maintenance of a highway

Greed's Invisible Hand

An Open Letter about Wealth and Money

Day 35: The Cloaked Invisibility

Greed has a negative connotation.
Greed is what allows for coexistence.
Self-interests are dependent on others,
and others depend on self-interests.
The philosophy of scarcity or abundance
is irrelevant,
for resources consumed endlessly will one day end.
This journey does not award participation trophies.
Everyone is a winner. Everyone is a loser.

*T*he Wealth of Nations.

This book was written back in the late 1700s by one Adam Smith in an attempt to study the art of decision-making, now presently known as *economics*. And in this book, he offered a hypothesis about your behavior through the observation of incentives.

The Invisible Hand of Greed.

Smith's interpretation uses the assumption that each individual is, in a way, selfish. Rather, that every person is motivated by his or her own desires. Even under the guise of helping others, there is usually a personal impetus, even if it is to simply make you feel good about yourself. Put loosely, "There is no such thing as a selfless good deed."

Smith argues that greed itself is the invisible motivator. I offer perhaps a slightly different spin on the context. There is no denying that you all must be greedy in some sense, and sometimes that may come at the cost of others.

I argue greed is always very apparent. Greed is just like a person, with its own mind, motivation, and perspective. Greed itself is not invisible. But the amount of control that Greed has in your life is Greed's invisible hand. Greed's invisible hand is the large or small, strong or delicate, prominent or faint influence in your life. Greed's hand can have a parasitic relationship with your soul or a mutual relationship with your soul. Greed's hand is a powerful yet invisible motivator, altering the way you choose to live your experience of Me compared to how you *want* to live your experience of Me. If you do not learn to control Greed, Greed will control you.

Balance Statement

Do you agree with Smith's conclusion on greed? Why or why not?

Checklist:

- If you won $1 million, what would you buy? Write it down.
- Identify a time when your self-interest intertwined with someone else's.
- Choose one community service project you can engage in this month.

Repetition is key to retention. Write your personal mantra that you believe reflects the treasure of wealth. You will repeat this mantra throughout the discussion of wealth.

Personal Mantra:

Write a time when you noticed Greed's presence in your life. How did you react?

Wealth

Day 36: Greed's Arrival

Wealth and richness are measured in units you assign.

Is it a currency?

Is it love?

Power?

Happiness?

You can be greedy with anything.

A commodity held in high value is susceptible to an equivalent level of greed.

The cost will be high.

Peace. Friendships. Confidence.

Wealth is no longer an asset. It is a blinded liability.

The endless search to fulfill the pit with disregard to mass accumulation.

It will never be enough.

reed makes an appearance when there is a desire to consistently acquire wealth. Greed's presence becomes uncontrollable when the journey to acquire more wealth clouds your essence and character. Your society has come up with the term "wealth" to dictate the accumulation of materialistic items that have a high value.

I suppose I have similar thoughts on wealth. I, too, believe that wealth is an accumulation of high-value items. So high in value that they are priceless. To me, those are things such as knowledge, love, happiness—commodities that no one can take away without your consent. Rather, they are not obligations that must be met in some sort of collateral-based parameter. There is nothing wrong with wanting to accumulate things, but if you acquire these things without remembering the experiences that make me truly enjoyable, I must beg the question: How wealthy are you, truly?

Your wealth commodity will always be within reach, but you will have to sacrifice in other areas. If you measure wealth by having more time for personal goals, you forgo time spent cultivating relationships. If you measure wealth by power, you may forgo enjoyable experiences that do not add value to your empire. This displays another economic concept called opportunity cost. The truth is wealth—just like everything, it seems—is a balancing act. Learning the art of balance lies in maximizing your individual wins while minimizing the sacrifices you must make to obtain your desires.

Balance Statement

What is your wealth commodity? Is it love? It is family time? Is it time with your children? Is it material assets and money? Is it travel?

Checklist:

- Write down a time when you wished for a seemingly limitless amount of a material possession.
- Reflect on an experience you felt incredibly lucky to be a part of. It can be a concert, time with family, or a cooking session with a loved one.
- Ask a colleague about their wealth commodity.

Personal Mantra:

Draw a treasure chest. What would be in your ideal treasure chest?

Wealth

Day 37: Greed's Currency

Astonishing, really, the things given up for collection of money.
You gave up your happiness for more money.
You gave up your dreams to get more money.
You valued what you brought to a relationship because of money;
conversely, what relationships you would engage in solely based off money.
Never happy. Never fulfilled. Never content.
Prolonged seeing the world.
Prolonged learning a new skill.
Prolonged acquiring an item you may have desired for a long time.
And suddenly Death comes.
And you, lowered into an identical grave.

W hile I have mentioned that wealth can be measured in accordance to the standards of your personal valuation system, I have observed over time that an increasingly popular wealth commodity is money. I'm not sure if I ever really planned for this to be a part of your experience of me. Forget part—a *necessity* of your experience of me. I thought everything had been provided on this planet Earth. I really never anticipated you, as a collective entity, to create something that you hold so much value for, something that rules everything in your life. When this concept of money was created, my purpose was suddenly reassigned to collect as much of this paper as possible, for apparently, that created your happiness. You might acquire possessions, people, status, and so many other dependencies to create "happiness" for you. But happiness comes from nothing other than yourself.

I was initially not sure how to react to this social concept. At first, I was impressed, for you managed to develop a whole social ecosystem based on value made from metal and paper. I mean, you can use goats as payment for only so long. What I had not accounted for was how prominent this concept became in your "understanding" of my purpose and your experience of me. My purpose became redefined to a number.

But then I contemplated a little more. I realized this system would have been inevitable. Humans are innovative, if anything. I realized money, or some valuation system, was necessary; to try to tell you otherwise would be unrealistic. You can't really understand what I, Life, am about if you are not alive. And sometimes, not having enough money to survive can make your death slow and quite painful. I suppose money does not make sense to me because I don't discriminate. My essence flows through whomever is chosen, regardless of their "money." But money can discriminate. And so can Greed.

Balance Statement

What are your goals regarding securing financial stability?

Checklist:

- Write two activities you have prolonged until you "earn more money."
- Start investing your money. If you are new to such an endeavor, take the first step and speak with a bank representative to learn about investing with bank-rated funds.
- Write down a comfortable earnings range (within this year, you can adjust for inflation over time).

Personal Mantra:

Pick a goal you have delayed in achieving because of money and set a deadline by which you will have accomplished that goal. Create a budget sheet and write areas in which you can save small amounts of money to reach your goal over time.

Day 38: Wealth's Freedom

Fear is a contagious infection.
Fear is a crutch.
Obtaining wealth out of fear is a mask for pain and problems to come.
To fill a hole with suitable materials requires fearlessness.
The most important commodity in this life is you.

Y ou can be wealthy and have little money. You can be poor and have only money.

While there is no denying money can buy you happiness to an extent—or at least for survival and even small comforts—there is a degree of honesty that you must hold yourself accountable to. There is a line where money, or any wealth commodity for that matter, becomes a crutch. This crutch turns into enslavement to an opiate disguised as an elixir to temporarily fill a hole that is yearning for a long-term solution. A solution that you simply do not wish to dedicate the time to accurately develop. If wealth remains a life-long crutch, you will never know what it is to walk. And wealth is not a crutch that can follow you beyond the grave.

When you get lowered into your grave, are you lowered any differently than the others around you? Will there be many people mourning the world's loss when they mourn you? Will you be proud of who you were? If you fear the answers to such questions, now is the time to ponder. Now is the time to make the change. But change only comes if you truly *want* to change.

Find the balance between monetary wealth and life wealth which makes life sustainable and enjoyable. Moderation will be the key to unlock the riches of your treasure chest.

My only warning, or food for thought, is that being wealthy by blatantly exploiting others is the worst kind of poor. Beware of Greed's invisible hand.

Balance Statement

How will you accumulate your wealth?

Checklist:

- Thank someone who has enriched your life and made your relationship feel valuable.
- Take a picture of your wealth commodity. Keep it on your nightstand.
- Give some of your wealth commodity away. Is it time? Volunteer one afternoon. Is it love? Do a random act of kindness for a stranger.

Personal Mantra:

Draw a scale. On one side, write commodities. On the other side, write sacrifices. How will you balance wealth in your life?

The Dormant Lion

An Open Letter about
Success and Redefining Yourself

Success

Day 39: The Eyes of the Lion

The jungle is a fascinating place.
Home to hundreds of creatures, vegetation, and foliage,
the jungle is one of many kingdoms.
Every realm a king rules,
the dwellers pay homage and respect.
The lion is a seemingly fit king of the jungle.
Leader of his pack, protector of kin, dutiful to his alpha responsibilities.
Enemies run in terror
from his strength.
The scouring scavenger
leers near the pride.
The scrounger senses opportunity in weakness.
The lion cannot meekly ask, "Can you please leave my family alone?"
For they hyena will cackle and taunt,
"Where is your dignity, Lion?"

L ions are so unbelievably commanding with their presence, that a whole movie was made about their circle of life from cub to king. Lions have mastered the art of leadership. They understand the crucial ingredient to success as a leader. The key to the lion's ability to assert power is in his being awake. That seems fairly apparent; a sleeping being has a difficult time asserting power.

I am not referring to physical consciousness. I am referring to the consciousness of the mind. A dormant mind is closed from reaching its full potential. Again, not a mind that is simply functioning in daily tasks, but a mind hungry for growth, starving for achievement, and disciplined to assert itself in manners necessary to achieve a desired outcome. The respect the lion commands is built from years of ruling the jungle. The power the lion possesses remains only as potent as the lion's conviction that he dictates the order of the jungle. The minute the lion's belief wavers, so does the loyalty of his constituents.

You are a ruler of a kingdom as well. And if you want to maintain the throne, you must be the lion of your kingdom. Your kingdom can contain all the riches, successes, passions, and happiness that your heart so desires. Unfortunately, I so rarely see humans, aware and formidable creations, sit upon the throne they so desperately crave. They are always missing something.

Believing in yourself.

But do not be disillusioned: Believing in yourself *alone,* is not enough.

Jungle Book

Is your mind awake or dormant?

Checklist:

- Sit somewhere quietly. Take five big shoulder rolls forward. Take five big shoulder rolls backward. Breathe deeply through this practice. Calm your mind. Focus your day.
- Write down three goals you would like to accomplish by the end of the month. It can be big or small—everything is a victory. Perhaps deep-clean the house, pay some bills, or visit an old friend.
- Watch a TED Talk that seems appealing to you.

Repetition is key to retention. Write your personal mantra that you believe reflects the treasure of success. You will repeat this mantra throughout the discussion of success.

Personal Mantra:

Write down how many browser pages your mind has open right now. Close two to three of them within the hour.

Success

Day 40: The Lion's Recipe

Success has tangibility.
The confusion lies in the classification: dream or success.
Failure, perseverance, gratitude, and tenacity.
Dedication, commitment, organization, and vision.
These are the main ingredients.
Luck and opportunity
are the seasonings.
The merging of success and dreams
are goals.
And what are goals, really,
if nothing but an event with a deadline?

The lion's recipe is not much of a secret. It has been told time and time again. While belief and faith are also key ingredients, success does not present itself because you believe it will. While the grocery list seems very long, you may find comfort in the reminder that success is very attainable. If you define success on your own terms, then you can always be successful, for you are striving for goals you charted. Often, I hear the words *success* and *dream* used interchangeably. I don't think success and dreams are the same thing.

Dreams are accomplishments you want, but would never put forth the effort to complete because you feel the cost of achieving this dream outweighs the benefit. Success, on the other hand, is very attainable. So long as you organize your success checklist, you will be successful you keep checking off those boxes. If you define success as meeting your goals, and define your goals as your dreams, you have inadvertently come up with a plan to successfully accomplish your dreams. The tricky part lies with the process of accomplishing the goals themselves. Ah, this is where the secret ingredient is put into the mix. And without this ingredient, all the other ingredients become useless.

Discipline.

Discipline is a very selective trait and does not present itself often in humankind by default. Therefore, many choose not to cultivate discipline because it is timely and requires a high amount of resource consumption. But now more than ever, discipline is an essential facet to your experience of me.

And a lack of discipline is a recipe for stagnation.

Jungle Book

What ingredients do you have for the recipe for success?

Checklist:

- Write down one trait you feel is missing from your recipe and focus on strengthening that trait.
- Write down one goal you would like to cultivate more discipline towards. Write a game plan that will help you become more disciplined regarding that goal.
- Write down an area you feel you have stagnated in. Reflect on potential solutions to change the tide.

Personal Mantra:

Pick one small goal. Strive for that goal for the whole month. Even if you fail, start again the next day. It can be making your bed daily, waking up at a certain time every day, or being punctual every day. Write that goal here.

_____

_____

_____

_____

_____

_____

_____

_____

_____

_____

_____

_____

_____

_____

Success

Day 41: The Lion's Slumber

The boundaries for your kingdom
shall be redefined numerous times.
As such, new opportunities will arise.
The world is limitless.
Degrees do not define careers.
Creativity is to be explored in any form.
Failure with love in the past
is not the love of the future.
Travel the roads of the Earth,
for they can sustain life.
What makes you come alive?
For you can be and do anything.
But be warned:
Challenges for the throne come often.
The hyena was always an insatiable animal.

For all of discipline's importance, I would argue that the biggest obstacle in the cultivation of discipline is a lack of structure. While the beauty of me is that I have no outline stating the right way to live, that is also my darkness. Self-imposed deadlines require an incredible amount of discipline, because your only competition is time.

Time is a deadline you cannot see. Death is the only guaranteed moment in Life. Time is the ultimate paradox. It is hard to wrap the mind around an invisible end, which makes life feel like an infinite moment. When something is infinite, it becomes less valuable, or at least overlooked in value. There is no urgency to complete anything by a seemingly non-existent deadline. However, the reality is that life is held to an imperceptible, ticking clock. And even though the clock is still ticking, there are no visible hands to tell you the time.

The scariest part about not knowing the time, or time's lack of structure, is having to think and do for yourself. It is easier to maneuver without structure when someone else is telling you what to do. This is often the reason young adults struggle so much. After years of having others think for them, using their mind on their own feels a lot like leaving a teenage couple to supervise themselves.

But here as a young adult, lies the first opportunity for your lion to prove himself as king. This is often the first of many experiences to define oneself. In this process of definition, the king gets to decide how to rule, whom to rule, and the boundaries of the kingdom. Regardless of where you are in this process, opposers and conflict will continue to rise. Every opposer will seem challenging in their own way. But the good news is much of the opposition will be self-inflicted, because many problems are self-inflicted. Since 99 percent of battle success comes from courage to face the fear, the results are often within your control.

Courage lies in the diligence to follow the solution properly to ensure the complete resolution of the problem. And the longer you wait, the more dormant the lion becomes, for there has been no call for the lion to wake and fulfill its duty.

Jungle Book

What does courage mean to you? Who do you think of when you read the word *courage*?

Checklist:

- Write a time when you met a self-imposed deadline.
- Write a time when you did not meet a self-imposed deadline.
- Write about the first time you became the lion of your own kingdom.

Personal Mantra:

Ask a mentor or older colleague about their thoughts on courage. How has their opinion of courage changed from now in comparison to ten years ago? Write your conversation highlights here.

Success

Day 42: Simba's Adolescence

Realism of goals is a peculiar sentiment.
Are you not all human?
Did you not start with the same stages
of crawling before walking?
Did you not start with the same
mashed food before solids?
Where was the question of realism?
The simple difference
is discipline.
Whether the goal be "normal" or "un normal",
the only hinderance
is you.

There will be many encouraging you to be more "realistic" in your goals. Make no mistake: suggesting a structured path is a form of caring. People just want to make sure you are okay. Often, only the positives of this path will be highlighted to keep more people down that "structured" path. Your world wants more people to be "normal" rather than pursing more difficult, personalized routes.

Accounting versus acting. Scientist versus singer. Doctor versus dancer. I never understood why goals have to be separated to "normal" and "unnormal", but I guess that is the way of your society. To me, goals are goals. If your happiness and joy lie within an "unnormal" realm, the only thing holding you back will be yourself, thus ceding your throne to someone else. If you want to be a musician, and you're berated with concerns such as "You will never make it," and you believe them, then you really did not give yourself a fighting chance, did you?

But even once you have claimed your throne, you are not done. That would be like saying once you have bought your house, you are done taking care of it. The maintenance of your throne is paramout in your long reign as ruler of your kingdom. Life, rather me, is never in equilibrium; thus, the upkeep process is constant. There will always be something to upheave the equilibrium, no matter how hard you try to make everything as perfect as you can.

One day, you will come to the realization that such perfection is impossible. To aim for perfection is a waste of time. I'm not sure if "perfect" has a universal meaning. You may believe that others have accomplished the perfection you so desperately desire. Or at least it seems they have significantly fewer challenges to their throne than you. That illusion is well encompassed in the phrase, "The grass is greener on the other side." It's easy to be susceptible to thinking that everyone else's experience of me is better than your own. The reality is that I am fluid in your journey.

Jungle Book

What was a dream you had that someone told you was unrealistic?

Checklist:

- Ponder: Do you desire to make that dream a goal? Or leave it as a dream?
- If you desire to make that dream a goal, set your phase one deadline.
- Take a moment for gratitude and pride. Tell yourself out loud: "I am enough. I have accomplished success. And I will continue to accomplish all I desire."

Personal Mantra:

Write your success checklist here. What do you need to make your successes a reality?

_____

_____

_____

_____

_____

_____

_____

_____

_____

_____

_____

_____

_____

_____

_____

_____

Success

Day 43: The Circle of Triumph

Decades are just markers for the average mileage.
Just a few examples of millions.
The Twenties have youth and energy, but are hard financially.
The Thirties have family and newfound stability
but are marred by stress to build a future.
The Forties have wealth and establishments
but are shackled by the demands of life.
The Fifties have freedom and money, but less energy.
What you have today will contribute to what you have tomorrow.
What you have tomorrow would have never been possible without what you did today.
Every decade is full of effort to work toward the goals you wanted to accomplish.
This race has free rein.
In start. In stop. In breaks.
Everyone is winging me. Everyone is winging Life.

On your quest for success, remember to stay focused and not blinded. Be wary when your desires become heavily influenced by others. The saddest part of making comparisons to others is the fact that when you work so hard for your future, you often forget to live in the present. And then once you have accomplished all you had worked for, you forget to enjoy to fruits of your labor because you are too consumed with what is happening next. All of this to impress others! Your future should be the vision you imagined; it is unwise to achieve success for others' sakes and miss the present moments. Too often, you forget to enjoy these moments because you think they are waste of time, that it delays the achievement of your success. I have some hard news:

You can do everything right, and still lose.

Achieving success is costly. Ambition can be costly—and sometimes without reward. My only suggestion is for there to be honest and realistic conversations about success and its pitfalls. This allows for more opportunities to learn from one another and hopefully make different mistakes. Parents so often want that for their children. I argue you can want that for the future and for yourself. The only way to make me better is to make yourselves better. And who knows? Maybe one day your open conversations will start a domino effect in all those you meet.

It may seem virtually impossible to fight and conquer the endless obstacles obstructing the creation of your perfect kingdom. But I disagree, for I present a different kind of war. It is more an art of war.

Each one of you starts with a blank canvas. As you draw more on the canvas, you will undoubtedly have more "mess-ups." These will be mistakes that you made, ruining the drawing you were aiming for. And yet, with each "mess-up," you will one day recognize that they make up your beautiful picture on your own canvas. A picture that you never anticipated you would create. That is why it is so captivatingly beautiful. The picture is your own creation. It started with expectations and ends with reality. A picture of your kingdom.

Jungle Book

What will you fill your kingdom of success with? Which territories do you want your kingdom to enter? Motherhood? Fame?

Checklist:

- Write about three hard battles in your life that you won.
- Write about three hard battles in your life that you lost.
- List five of your victory trophies. Maybe they are your children, your friends, your dreams, etc.

Personal Mantra:

If your life could be woven into a quilt, what parts of your life would be woven in? What picture do you envision for such a piece of artwork? Draw your tapestry and date the picture. Five years from now, draw the tapestry again. Then, compare the drawings.

The Misnomer

An Open Letter about Dreams

Day 44: Society's Mistake

Misnomer, noun:
the misnaming of a person in a legal instrument.
Dream, noun:
a strongly desired goal or purpose.
How interesting.
The word dream is literally defined as a goal or purpose.
The cloud shadowing the potential of achievability is, in fact, the dreamer's.

You know, if people properly classified things, you wouldn't need the word *misnomer* in the dictionary. I suppose misnomers are there simply because society's interpretation of a word tends to vary from the actual definition. I think dreams have fallen prey to this oversight. The word *dream* is a misnomer because the definition of dream in the dictionary compared to society's interpretation is extremely varied. If we take society's interpretation and combine it with the dictionary definition, the definition of dream would be more along the lines of "an achievable goal that is often left unfulfilled because of varied circumstances; a belief of the dream's unattainability due to the perceived outlandish requirements to obtain the dream." Maybe not a definition at all, but perhaps more of a philosophy.

It is society's interpretation of the word *dream* that is the misnomer. Society associates dreams with being "unrealistic". But dreams, by all accounts of the true definition, are not unrealistic. Perhaps the bigger question is where the idea of being "unrealistic" came from. After all, that altered perception must come from some experience or observation leading to such a conclusion. After much research, I have come to the conclusion that the difference between a dream and a success can be boiled down to two words.

Mediocrity and isolation.

Dream Chart

How do you define *dream*?

Checklist:

- Write a dream you have that aligns with your definition of *dream*.
- Write a dream you have that aligns with society's definition of *dream*.
- Ask a loved one about a dream they pursued.

Repetition is key to retention. Write your personal mantra that you believe reflects the treasure of dreams. You will repeat this mantra throughout the discussion of dreams.

Personal Mantra:

Ask a young child what they want to be when they grow up and why. Write their response. Write your dream from that same age. Then write your dreams now. Are they the same, or drastically different?

Day 45: The Self-Help Lies

All books of the self discuss the same traits
but veil the truth.
Not all these traits work.
There is no one-size-fits-all.
In truth,
the only universal trait
is personal analysis.
Vision is not always needed when there is flexibility.
Humility is attractive but not imperative.
Determination is sometimes just stubbornness.
Perseverance may be needed sparingly.
And comparison to others is futile.
For dreams are not always earned.
But the joke is always
on the ones who do not even start.

I f you have read a self-help book before, the topics and traits discussed are pretty similar across the board. I think that is why I researched so intensely on what was *not* there. Why is it that so few accomplish their dreams despite all the guidance available? I realized, in junction with mediocrity and isolation, the biggest obstacle in achieving your dreams is the constant comparison of yourself to others.

Mediocrity and isolation both play a pivotal role in not only achieving your dream but also understanding what shall be required from you in this pursuit. Time spent comparing is a waste. It will seem that some people worked much harder for their dream than you did, while others did significantly less but still accomplished them with such intensity that it transcended expectations. But what others do does not matter. They are not the ones trying to achieve your dreams. You are. All that matters for you is to keep your eyes on the prize.

You can make no mistakes, and still lose. You can do nothing right, and still win. And it may seem unfair, the way others' seem to do nothing right and succeed, or why some of the best people have the most rotten luck. I never said I was fair, and there is no amount of analysis that will help you determine why I am unfair. I spent a lot of time pondering why people expended time comparing themselves to others. I realized it is in the examination of mediocrity's and isolation's roles that explains why comparison to others is so prevalent despite its ineffectiveness.

Dream Chart

How many times a day do you compare yourself to someone else? When was the last time you did so and why?

Checklist:

- Next time you compare yourself to someone, stop and say aloud, "I am proud of myself, and I am pretty freaking cool."
- Tell someone why you admire them.
- Thank a role model for how they have impacted your life.

Personal Mantra:

Take a break from a social media outlet for three days. Write how you feel after the hiatus, and how your mind feels.

Day 46: Mediocrity

To blame technology would be too easy.
Technology is merely a tool.
It is with the wielder the tool's destiny lies.
Laziness has stemmed from using the tool, yes,
but the tool has also added efficiency.
It has done its job well.
Convenience is a new plague;
immediate satisfaction of the now.
A happy relationship, now.
Achievement of social and intellectual status, now.
This is the fault of society.
For have you forgotten the tool of time?

N ow comes the part of the self-help book that is unpleasant, because it highlights self-accountability. And everyone loves the truth until it's about them. Dreams are not mediocre goals. But, in your society, mediocrity is becoming increasingly celebrated, or tolerated at least. As a collective entity, the social order has lowered their standards. When someone does something that they should be doing, generally the bare minimum, the populace celebrates the work because it's above and beyond these lowered expectations. This has created a culture of satisfaction in complacency. Comfortable in the celebration of achievements that are nothing more than ordinary. What is the need to "dream big" when even the simplest of responsibilities are rejoiced, commended even? Since such small acts become celebrated, everyone can be a winner! That sentiment is so unbelievably unworkable, it almost hurts.

You have forgotten how to lose.

Nothing motivates you to work harder, innovate more, and envision better possibilities than the desire to win. But nothing motivates the dream of your individual success better than losing. It is hard to have great dreams when the definition of *greatness* has been altered to meet the definition of *average*. Dreams do not appear overnight. Dreams take time. And sadly, instead of time being an understood factor of achievement, it has been morphed into an obstacle and deterrent for pursing said achievement.

The ripple effect of lowering standards has created the ability to get away with a subpar performance, instantly gratified by a tumultuous applause, leaving no need, nor mindfulness, to improve. It becomes much more difficult to live life when you find no purpose. It's hard to find purpose when you don't have to work to achieve all your aspirations within the limited time you and I share. For when temporary effort is given, temporary satisfaction will follow.

Dream Chart

When do you put forth mediocre work? Why do you think that is?

Checklist:

- Write about a time when you gave a mediocre performance due to lack of interest.
- Write about a time when you gave 100 percent of your ability to something you were interested in.
- Write about a time when you gave 100 percent of your ability to something you were not interested in.

Personal Mantra:

Write a time when technology improved efficiency in your life. Write a time when your dependence on technology made you lazy.

_____

_____

_____

_____

_____

_____

_____

_____

_____

_____

_____

_____

_____

_____

_____

Day 47: Isolation

Humans have been great.
Humans are great.
Humans can be great.
Such proof lies throughout history.
Proof that mankind possesses the capability
to mold the future.
Caught between breaking barriers
and a world shackled to indulgence,
nothing worth having comes easy.
Nothing.
To be great,
you must work for it.
You must sacrifice for it.
Experience the failure.
Experience the frustration.
To be something more than your existence requires action beyond existing.

The human race is living more and more unfulfilled every day. This new threat to living, in which complacency has become the new normal, must change. Don't misunderstand me. I am not oblivious to the roadblocks in dream achievement. Time, energy, money, resources, and lack of guidance are all major roadblocks. The trick then is obviously figuring a way to get over and around said roadblocks. The biggest question is: How?

No one achieves their dreams alone.

Sometimes you may feel like a fool for pursuing goals and giving so much to them when it seems no one else cares. People may make fun of you or give you false support. Pay no mind to that. Your focus is to make sure you accomplish your goal. Because in the end, it's your satisfaction that matters, not anyone else's. I can tell you for a fact that the only entity that sets the parameters of dreams being "too big", is yourself.

But isolation, or the lack of vocalizing your desires and dreams to others, is a big mistake. There will be plenty of people who have walked similar paths as you and can help. Perhaps they may offer guidance to a more strategic pathway to reach your destination. Perhaps they can offer much-needed support. Your attitude plays a large role, but it's not enough. Isolation is the best way to make sure your dreams never see the light of day.

Dream Chart

Have you ever vocalized your dream to someone who can help make it a reality?

Checklist:

- Find someone who works in the field of your dream. Reach out to them and ask if they can spare time to speak with you. Networking is part of dream achievement as much as it is with employment.
- Identify a small handful of people you trust who are genuinely supportive of your dreams. Update these people on your dreams and how you're attempting to achieve them.
- Show kindness to yourself. Especially in times of failure. Say one positive statement any time a harsh one enters your mind. What's one you can say right now?

Personal Mantra:

Find a quote you resonate with by someone who has achieved a dream you see for yourself. Frame it.

Day 48: Faithfulness in Competition

By doing something small in the present,
you can drastically change the future.
Starving for this goal,
breathing only the success of this goal,
drowning so badly
to the point where not meeting this goal is an utter ruin to your quality of life—
only then will you gather whatever resources are needed
to make this dream a reality.
Continual small steps
will reach the destination quicker than realized.
A quick fix is just that: a quick fix.
It is your decision to achieve your goals with honesty and integrity.

*C*ompetition.

Some say I am not. Some say I am. The good and bad news: both are wrong.

Individually, you have your own journey, but you do share many experiences of me with others. There are only so many resources for you to meet your needs. Time, energy, money, love, everything. Those resources are not found in perfect amounts to meet every single person's desires and needs. Many of you have the same goals. Resources do deplete. And while your worth is not contingent on the time frame in which you achieve your goals, the quicker you learn about your competition, the sooner you can obtain the necessary resources to achieve your dreams.

There is one resource that you can find in abundance, should you choose to provide it in abundance: the resource of faith. It's irrelevant who does or does not believe in you. No one can chew for you. If you don't chew for yourself, your body starves to death. You will starve your dream if you rely on others to feed it.

I hope you dream endlessly, for there is no finish line in dreaming. Dreaming's splendor lies in dream's subjectivity. Dreaming is what makes *you* come alive. So, whether you dream big or small, dream to achieve. Dream to accomplish. Believe in yourself to dream. And above all, remember, you are the captain of all your dreams' success.

Dream Chart

Which definition of *dream* will you chose to follow: yours or society's?

Checklist:

- Write five resources you will need to achieve your dreams. Be specific.
- Look in the mirror. Smile at yourself and say, "I have faith in you."
- Set aside ten minutes every day this week. Sit quietly in a corner and breathe deeply. Visualize your dream and your achievement of that dream.

Personal Mantra:

Draw a dreamcatcher. Draw five dreams the dreamcatcher caught. Prioritize those dreams from one to five—one being most pressing to accomplish, five being least pressing to accomplish.

The Cry of the Phoenix

An Open Letter about Loss and Death

Loss and Death

Day 49: Cloaked Darkness

Your breath sucked out of your soul,
creating a suffocating bubble of poisonous air.
The world has lost color,
the stars their brilliance.
Vitality is clouded
by a dull and thumping gray haze.
You walk by Happiness
without recognition.
You have forgotten her taste, her smell, her love.
For all you recognize now?
Despair.

I imagine if Despair could be personified, the description of a cloaked, faceless figure would more than suffice. I imagine Despair's symbolism simply: A dark, thunderous, gloomy cloud with turmoil visible only to you. And this cloud is unlike normal rain clouds. This cloud is chilling, filled with acidic rain, and provides no nurture. This cloud enters your life when you have experienced loss or death. The cloud brews from feelings that are inevitable, feelings that come from experiences that are inevitable. As such, anguish, grief, and sadness can still creep up even if everything "seems" to be going well.

Often when you see this cloud, it's because something is missing. You are not well. But your interpretation of *well* is different than your colleagues' interpretation of *well*. It's different than your parents' interpretation. Than your children's. Maybe you have a good job, a great family, wonderful friends, but you feel no purpose in your existence. You are not entirely well, then. And it is not happiness itself that is missing; no, it is the lack of knowing what makes you happy which allows this cloud into your abode. When something is missing, it means it is lost. You may find it again. You may not.

You will lose a lot on our journey together. Happiness, love, wealth, the list is endless. Life, me, cannot happen without loss. I also cannot happen without death.

I often feel there is a misconception that loss and death are only put into context regarding people. But loss and death can occur with anything in any facet of your existence.

Eulogy

What images run through your mind when you reflect on the hard times in your life?

Checklist:

- Write a time when negative images clouded your mind.
- Write your interpretation of "doing well."
- If you are ready, make an appointment with a mental health professional. Even if you are doing well.

Repetition is key to retention. Write your personal mantra that you believe reflects the treasure of loss and death. You will repeat this mantra throughout the discussion of loss and death.

Personal Mantra:

Draw your happy place. Is it a beach? The mountains? A cabin in the woods? Visualize that place every night before you sleep.

Loss and Death

Day 50: Not One and the Same

Loss breeds loneliness;
occasionally,
before such a loss is even realized.
Emptiness grows.
The sense of lost enhanced.
Prisoner of your mind.
But this is to be expected
as well as death.
And death is the cloud's oxygen.

I do not believe loss and death are the same thing. Loss is often a checkpoint that people reach before they either head toward death or turn back. With loss, there is a chance of recovery. Sometimes, situations arise where you feel a temporary absence of a person, feeling, or essence. But when there is no recovery, just permanent loss, that is death.

You can lose passion. You can lose freedom. You can lose love. You can lose a loved one.

Your passion can die. Your freedom can die. A loved one's essence and legacy can die. Love for someone can die. You can die.

The death I am referring to is different than my counterpart, who happens to be a third party like me.

The death I am referring to is permanent departure. Nothing is more degrading and saddening, or hardening than this blow to the chest. It rips your heart into shreds, you breathe nothing but the blood spilling out of when you realize a permanent loss of something that once gave you life. What once made your room brighter, your eyes sparkle, and your laugh louder is now gone. Forever. It sounds like I am describing love, but death is not so different from love. Any kind of death cannot come without love, and it is arguable which one is kinder.

There is nothing quite like the death of your innocence by realizing the ugliness that exists among humanity and the world. There is nothing quite like the death of your youthful rebellion when you embrace the societal standards you once fought so hard against.

But this will all happen.

Eulogy

What do you think about loss and death? Write from your heart.

Checklist:

- What is something you have lost? Write it down.
- What is something of yours that has died? Write it down.
- Ask a friend what their thoughts are on loss and death. Have a discussion.

Personal Mantra:

Write a letter to someone you lost in the past but still want to find your way back to.

Loss and Death

Day 51: Born of Fire

Emptiness has a high endurance.
Coping requires dirty hands,
a hard job;
but without cleansing,
the dirt hardens as sadness stays well-fed,
haunting.
The sun still rises and sets.
The calendar moves forward.
Heed this solace.
You can be reborn from your ashes.

While I never found an easy symbol to allude for this rebirth, I feel the phoenix adequately suffices. For the phoenix is burned from its own fire and reborn from its own ashes. Much like Fawkes, you, too, will be burned by your own fires. Burned by the fires of your passions. Burned by your fires of love. Burned by the fires of risks and failures. These ashes provide two opportunities: remain as a collection of ash piles or be reborn. Reborn to find new passion. Reborn to learn to love again. Reborn to readjust the terms you want to embrace both me and Death. An opportunity for your phoenix to rise and soar.

Make no mistake—you will collect hundreds of ash piles. And with each ash pile, the two opportunities will present themselves. It will seem like a never-ending job of cleaning up. Many times, you will do everything you can to be reborn, only to burn again almost immediately. You will sit in your ashes, too devastated by their destruction to even stand. This will happen when you are searching for solutions to an unknown problem. You will ask two questions repeatedly while your eyes seethe with anger, voice dry from all the screaming.

Why bother with the process of rebirth to only have to be reborn repeatedly?

How many times will the process of rebirth happen?

Eulogy

Have you had a phoenix-like experience in your life before?

Checklist:

- Write a time when you rose from your ashes.
- Write a time when you have let an ash pile just sit, with no rebirth.
- Write what current struggle you are going through, from which a phoenix will rise from one day.

Personal Mantra:

Draw and color your phoenix.

Loss and Death

Day 52: No Phoenix Is the Same

Time is the moral of the story.
Time holds lessons of growth.
Time holds opportunities of success and change.
This life is nothing more than a blink of an eye.
Every loss, every death, a new you to rise.
A kinder you.
A humbler you.
Perhaps sadder.
Optimist turned realist.
It is the nature of things.
Nothing lasts forever.

There is a lot more that unites your species than divides. Both loss and death are painful and, ironically, perhaps the most unifying experience that everyone must go through. You all sit at the world table with your individual ash piles and phoenixes. The funny thing about man is despite the many similarities you share with all the guests at the table, you seem to focus only on the differences. Some will fail to notice that each person has ash piles. Others will focus on comparing their number of ash piles to everyone else's. Regardless of the fact that everyone there has at least one phoenix, the concern becomes the color of the phoenixes instead of the realization that every single person at this table has had some kind of rebirth.

Humans share this universal truth: Every single human creation is working toward the universal goal of finding their place in my puzzle before it is time to pay the piper. It is in that unified experience that allows you to fit together in this grand puzzle that I am. Your puzzle piece, while different and unique, is meant to be shared with the other puzzle pieces. Without your piece, the puzzle cannot be complete. That holds true for *all* my puzzle pieces. While I do not expect you as an individual to like every single puzzle piece, to view that piece as anything less than a part of my puzzle is unacceptable. What is even more outrageous is when you accept a person after they have departed. Death is not an excuse for fake kindness, sympathy, or respect.

Eulogy

What would you share at the world table? What is a difficulty you often face?

Checklist:

- Sit with a group of trusted friends. Ask them about one experience that changed their lives.
- Ask these same friends, "What do you want from life?"
- Write down what *you* want from life. It's okay to be vulnerable with this.

Personal Mantra:

Draw your puzzle piece. What is it shaped like? What color is it? What are the ridges like?

Loss and Death

Day 53: Dearly Departed

You may not get everything you want in this life.
If you died today, there will be plenty that you wished you could have accomplished.
Through no fault of your own, you did not get to.
Though Death is predictable,
there is a loophole enabling you to live beyond your decay.
To truly stay alive beyond your physical body,
embody what you want to be remembered as today.
Legacy is a consequence of character.
When your death is honored,
you do not get to hear what people say about you.
All you can do is hope
you were the kind of person that
the positive things said about you
were true.

There is a very common saying: "Do not pity the dead, pity the living." And while there is some truth to that statement, I think there are many times that the dead *should* be pitied. I think the dead should be pitied when the memory and legacy left behind is not one of happiness or peace or anything favorable. Too many have forgotten time's nature—"later" is not always promised.

I loathe that word. *Later*. It is used as an excuse to put off what should be done now, further supporting this illusion of infinite time. When Death comes, there are no pit stops; thus, you can't tell someone what you wanted to say but failed to do so when you were alive. The time to express love, appreciation, and desire is now. The time to do is *now*. History cannot be rewritten. Anything you do will be forever etched in history, and anything you do not accomplish will be lost with you.

Death is never truly the end. You can live as long as you want. You live through your acts of kindness. You live through memories. You live through your spirit, kindling warm fires to all who have met you. For it is your impact that on others that speak the immeasurable volumes of your story. Your story becomes your legacy. And you live on through your legacy.

Eulogy

What will your story look like?

Checklist:

- Tell someone you love them today.
- Let go of a grudge and accept an apology today.
- Seek forgiveness for a mistake you made today.

Personal Mantra:

What are three qualities you want to be remembered by? Write them down.

Loss and Death

Day 54: Legacy's Truth

The legacy of mankind,
is passed on through generations.
How you care for your children,
Advances in technology, medicine, and science,
Political ideologies and social revolutions
which have shaped the world.

Strangers remember compassion.
Friends remember laughter.
And the truth about legacy,
is that big or small,
your contributions to this world matter.

There is really no reason to be scared. Of Death, that is. I think the real reason you fear Death so much is because you fear you will be forgotten. That matter is up to you. I will forewarn you, though. For the most part, everyone becomes forgotten at some point. This is not because you lack importance or value. It is simply how the human brain works. As stories get passed down, information is bound to be lost. If you want to be remembered longer, my suggestion is to be someone worth remembering for a long time.

Despite these counsels, am I suggesting you live every waking moment as if it is your last? No, for that is stressful as well. I am merely attempting to impress upon you that our time together is short. I also hope you discover the importance of gratitude—not as a reminder that things could be worse, but as a reminder for all that you have and will overcome in our time together. Because for the living, Death is a powerful teacher. Not so much to mourn what you lost, but to appreciate what you have now. It seems that people come to appreciate and celebrate me as soon as I am gone.

You are in this world *now*. A life of judgment and fear is not a memorable life; it crushes any hope for a legacy. While the idea of physical immortality is laughable to me, I do find the idea of living forever quite achievable. Maybe your name gets lost, but the essence of your contribution to the world has a domino effect. And in the end, that is what really matters.

Eulogy

What will be your domino effect?

Checklist:

- Say ten things you are grateful for today.
- Write five qualities of yours that you are grateful for.
- Tell someone why you are grateful for their presence in your life.

Personal Mantra:

Write a eulogy you would want to hear at your funeral. Then ask a friend how honest that eulogy is. Highlight what changes you may need to make in your life to ensure the eulogy you wrote is an honest one.

The Man-Made Sunrise

An Open Letter about Happiness

Happiness

Day 55: Good Morning, Sunshine

As the moon finishes his shift within the hemisphere,
his colleague, the sun, walks toward the horizon.
As the sun's smile radiates, the workplace slowly begins to operate,
the cogs groaning as they are started, the smells and sounds of life
filling the peaceful silence the moon left behind.
Some days, the sun's smile is subdued or clouded,
but every day starts with this graced force of nature,
the sun's rising uncontrollable.
The weather conducting the day's orchestras.

The sun aids in the growth of crops, illuminates pathways, and provides warmth. It cannot, however, provide these same functions within yourself. When there is a lack of a natural resource, man makes a version of it—accurately coined "man-made." Your sun is man-made, rather self-made, to permeate throughout your life, aiding in your personal growth, illuminating other perspectives, and is a provider of happiness.

Here's the catch: You have complete control as to when your sun rises and when your sun sets. You also control if your sun rises again once it has set. It is a matter of many experiences, a process of trial and error, that stem the conditions in determining if the rising and setting is habitual, patterned, spontaneous, or conditional. As many of you will find out, generally the hard way, complete freedom over something often sounds much better than the actual experience of being given the reins with no restrictions. The only way you learn to control this freedom is when you've incurred a negative consequence after going a little too far.

Nature Journal

How do you feel when the sun basks on your face?

Checklist:

- Spend ten minutes at a park and just enjoy the sun.
- Go on a hike this month.
- Do an activity with a friend that brings you both happiness and laughter.

Repetition is key to retention. Write your personal mantra that you believe reflects the treasure of happiness. You will repeat this mantra throughout the discussion of happiness.

Personal Mantra:

Write three activities that make your sun radiate.

_____

_____

_____

_____

_____

_____

_____

_____

_____

_____

_____

_____

_____

_____

_____

Happiness

Day 56: Rain or Shine

Happiness is a journey, no doubt.
A long journey indeed, for routes fade.
Directions need to be changed. There are no mileage markers.
The pit stops do not provide rest,
for the sun disappears for a while, a seemingly everlasting inescapable gloominess.
The rain falls, with continuous downpour, no rays of light in sight.
The water drenches and submerges, cold to the touch.
But it was never about braving the rain.
It was always about the rainbow.

Y ou may be curious as to why your sun needs to be controlled. It is not your sun itself that needs to be controlled or monitored. It is the rationalizations behind the rising and setting of your sun that need to be dissected.

Is your happiness dependent on short-term or long-term vision?

Do the opinions of others determine how happy you are?

Do you know how to find happiness in even the darkest of times?

There are periods when your sun stays clouded for a while. The long duration of rain, or gloom, inhibits your sun's ability to shine. However, let me be clear: There is nothing wrong with rain, for that is as much a part of your sunrise as the sun. Rain is inevitable, and without rain, crops cannot grow.

Just like the crops, you, too, need both the sun and the rain. The rainbow is the most beautiful and captivating sight, but it is a result of the harmony of the rain and sun. The appreciation for the sun grows in great magnitude after a long period of rain, but that renewed appreciation would have never occurred if you had not lost the sun at some point.

Nature Journal

Have you experienced periods of rain on your quest for happiness? If so, how did you handle them?

Checklist:

- Write down an activity that makes you happy.
- Write down your feelings about that experience.
- Write down one of your coping mechanisms for periods of rain.

Personal Mantra:

Draw a tree. You're going to create a happiness tree using the activity from the checklist. Write that activity at the top. Create a branch for each feeling the activity gives you. Dig a little deeper. Why does that activity make you happy? Does the activity make you feel safe? Is it an expression of freedom? Write down your thoughts.

Happiness

Day 57: The Right Journey

Happiness is a journey.
There is no right route.
All roads lead to Rome,
it is simply a matter of
finding which road works for you,
in this moment.
Happiness cannot be forced.
Happiness can only be discovered,
unraveled, unearthed
from within.
Everlasting evolvement
ensures redirection.
Permanence in happiness
is contentment.

Happiness is a journey comprised of routing and rerouting. True happiness stems from a need, a yearn to have all aspects of your life in peaceful cohesion, and your willingness to do anything to find it. This journey, like most, is comprised of nothing but cycles of trial-and-error. The question always thumping in the back of the mind is: How do you know you have found the right route? Ah, that is an intriguing question.

While I do not believe I have found the right answer, I do think I have found a valid one. I think one of the biggest misconceptions you have about happiness is you believe happiness is found on the route where there is only sun and no rain. The right route reveals your *strategy* for tolerating the rain during and after the storm and, in time, eventually appreciating the rain. The right route is where you know how to bring your sun back after you have endured the rain.

If you are lucky, one day you will be able to stop your trial and error. You have reached your destination. You will stretch, breathe deeply, and let your face bask in the familiar presence of your sun. You will look around and see all the parts of your journey—the good, the bad, and the ugly—have been sun-kissed, for those moments will forever be a part of you. And when you reach your destination, you will realize your sun is everything *you* imagined.

Its shape took the form you thought it would, not the shape others described to you. Its degree of brilliance is set to your comfort level. The rays are as bright as you thought they would be, illuminating your most prized possessions. All materials occupying your destination are there by your desire. Anything others guaranteed would be at your destination are elsewhere, unless you gladly allowed them to occupy space at your destination.

Finally, all is well.

Nature Journal

What is your right route to happiness? How can you get there?

Checklist:

- Watch the sunrise once this week.
- Meditate while listening to the sound of rain (if it isn't raining, you can listen on your phone).
- Next time you have a difficult situation, take ten deep breaths. Then answer the question, "How can I bring my sun into this situation?"

Personal Mantra:

Draw a landscape that brings contentment to your mind. In other words, draw your happy place.

Happiness

Day 58: Hitchhikers

Music extends her hand
as she saves the listener from their own prison.
Music temporarily makes herself visible.
With a fleeting glance at Music's face doth come the reminder.
Gratitude and grace, for hearing is indeed the kindest of blessings.
Sadness and fear cower away
as the thunderous sound of singing fills the air.
The air is in joyous unison,
in joyous harmony,
and, if only for a moment, in joyous peace.

The journey to happiness is impossible without hitchhikers. These hitchhikers always impart the gift of memories because that is part of their job description. These hitchhikers, you thought, were various people meant to keep the journey bearable, fun even. But hitchhikers have a mission. Just like any secret agent, these "hitchhikers" are one person, just with various disguises.

Joy is literally a breath of fresh air. Not only does Joy's breeze refresh your mind, but Joy comes in many forms. Every time one of these hitchhikers joins you, it is actually Joy disguised. But she is with you for only a short time, so it is wise to breathe her air as deeply and as long as you can when in her presence. Joy has various disguises because her disguises resonate differently, depending on the person.

With Joy, conversations flow endlessly and easily. Your combined laughter is loud and infectious, to the point where your face hurts from smiling so much. Joy gives you a parting souvenir each time you interact. Those souvenirs are memories of Joy. And it is in these memories, small but blissful moments, that your smile widens, your giggle turns into a chuckle, and you remember why the whole journey to happiness was worth it in the first place.

Nature Journal

How many times have you picked up the hitchhiker, Joy? Is Joy in your life now? Why or why not?

Checklist:

- Write down a memory when you felt Joy's presence.
- What color represents Joy to you? Place that color in two places in your home.
- Show some appreciation. Compliment someone on their smile.

Personal Mantra:

If you were Joy, what parting souvenir would you give?

Happiness

Day 59: Joy's Smile

Joy is a reminder to "stop and smell the roses."
The roses are "it" factors,
allowing for life in the present.
The intoxicating scent of the roses breathes life to the present.
And, for just a moment,
the world falls away.
Senses heightened,
the out-of-body
euphoric experience.

J oy is often overlooked because her effect and presence are small and temporary; often, you don't think much of her contribution. You just want to reach the destination by any means necessary. And while arriving to the destination is important, your arrival would not have been possible without Joy. For while the journey for happiness is found within, it does get lonely. And the work is so hard, but Joy makes this work a little more bearable. Joy is that thing that gives you goosebumps, where you feel most united with your soul—all that makes life worth living such as music, art, pottery, cooking, poetry, writing, singing.

Perhaps these things make life worth living because they can unite so many differences together, and, if but for a moment, those differences become immaterial. Many incorrectly discern experiences of Joy as a "hobby." A hobby is something you do if you have spare time. But Joy is something you *must* make time for no matter what. Joy is an integral part of me that makes your experience of me uniquely enjoyable for you. Without Joy, your overall happiness can't possibly be at its maximum potential. Perhaps it truly was in the small details that your journey came together.

Nature Journal

What is one of your hobbies? Does it bring Joy into your life?

Checklist:

- Get back to an activity you enjoyed from your youth that you let go of over time.
- Pick one current hobby. Make it a moment of Joy for five to ten minutes daily.
- Bake a favorite pastry or cook a favorite meal from scratch this week. Consider sharing this food with a friend.

Personal Mantra:

Draw a vase and fill it with ten roses. On each rose, label an activity you get Joy from. You can incorporate any of these activities into your everyday life.

Happiness

Day 60: The Self-Made Playlist

Hans Zimmer, Elysium.
Above and Beyond, Treasure.
Papon, Jiyein Kyun.
Porter Robinson, Language.
Imogen Heap, Hide-and-Seek.
NF, This is all I have.
Evvy, Collide.
Switchfoot, Dare You to Move.
Seven Lions, Freesol.

Your journey of happiness will often be questioned by others. Happiness, the kind that comes from within, does not bode well for business. Humans are very simplistic in their needs to survive. You do not waver much from these necessities, and that does not sell very well. To overcome this problem, much of commerce's prosperity comes from advertising discretionary items as needs. Many will validate happiness through acquiring items, thus making you "happy" by societal standards. The most freeing part of reaching your destination is dictating your needs and wants unrelated of how they fit within society's parameters of "happiness." Once you have accomplished this, you are no longer a viable customer for the business of easy misguidance on routes that are nothing more than a dead end.

Your destination will be at the end of the route you chose both with and without guidance from others, like a self-made song playlist. Others may have exposed you to different music, but you get to pick which songs make it to your playlist. There will be no doubt in your mind once you start on this route. This path was for you because, finally, you no longer feel lost. Once you have reached your destination, you live in harmony with the weather. You prepare for rain and appreciate the rain. You see your rainbows, and smile. And every now and then, you catch a glimpse of the souvenir Joy gave you and appreciate the memory of her refreshing presence.

Nature Journal

What is your self-made playlist?

Checklist:

- Frame a picture that brings happiness. It can be of nature, family, friends, pets, etc.
- Smile for thirty seconds. Then laugh for thirty seconds. (If you need inspiration, pull up your favorite video clips or memes.) Write how long you end up laughing for.
- Ask a loved one about their moments of Joy. Then ask if they have found their route to happiness.

Personal Mantra:

What songs spell happiness for you? If music isn't your thing, how would you spell happiness in the item that brings you Joy (movies, podcasts, shows, festivals, foods, etc.)?

MY CONCLUSION

As you walk through time, your understanding will hit you like a tidal wave. This is why I do not come with a manual. You will learn to create your own everything. Your own legacy. Your own thoughts. Your own words. Your own actions. Your own dreams.

This will all come when you must repeatedly redefine who you are and who you want to be. Your throne will overlook a kingdom that you built from scratch, a kingdom filled with all your successes and failures. And then, when it is time for your kingdom's light to end, your canvas will display your own tale of battles and adventures. A story that will inspire some. Bring comfort to some. Be a reality check for some.

Nonetheless, your artwork will grace my throne room forever. And when the reign of your kingdom ends, your canvas will be woven into a tapestry made up of thousands of other art pieces. And when I cease to exist, the tapestry will be complete for this world.

As the sun sets permanently on this beautiful park called Earth, my last moments will be spent gazing at this massive tapestry, all the stories told with vibrant colors captivated so beautifully by the sun's rays. My last memory will be of all my reflections, and I cannot wait to see your artwork when it is time.

As you have read these letters, you will both agree and disagree with what has been narrated. History has proven that the same event can have entirely different meanings to different people. Many wars, both real and myth, were started because of a man's desire for a woman. The story could leave you with the conclusion that women are so powerful that to unleash such a power could leave a new world of possibilities. Or, you could conclude that women are demons whose beautiful power should be controlled. You could construe the argument that the failures of men are exactly why men should not be leading.

Or, that the failures of men have allowed the improvement of societies over time.

I challenge you to think about *your* interpretation of me currently, and then what you want your parting interpretation to be when you die. Desires and fears will vary from creation to creation.

Many say I am all about the journey to get to my counterpart, Death. Your individual adventure is comprised of many journeys. And each journey is filled with options. And every option leads you down another path for you to choose to walk. You and I do not share just one journey. All those journeys molded together create your unique life.

But in your uniqueness, there are some commonalities throughout civilizations. I think you call them clichés. I find that not all the time, but often, clichés hold such wisdom in their simplicity. Those statements hold truth through time, shifts in generations, and changes in trends. For some things are universally shared in their happenings.

But for all the happenings, whether universal or individual, I am so grateful to be a part of them. The greatest experiences I have are with you. My fellow friends, my greatest colleagues, leading me on the most amazing adventures. I am glad for every moment I get to spend with you. I am not the greatest gift to you. *You* are the greatest gift to me.

Thank you, my most cherished prize.

Sincerely,

Life

ACKNOWLEDGMENTS

I would like to thank my parents, but especially my dad, who was a beta reader and editor.

I would also like to thank my best friend Brian and my sister Komal, who both took the time to read my book and give me feedback and patiently dealt with all my thoughts and writing craziness.

I would also like to thank Melinda Martin, who gave me a beautifully designed book inside and out.

Words cannot express how grateful I am to all those who have supported me and believed in me to make my dream a goal, and then my goal a reality. I am forever grateful.

ABOUT THE AUTHOR

Poonum Desai started her writing career in her early twenties after finishing her master's in public policy. She discovered her interest in writing after she originally picked up writing as a hobby to deal with the joys of adulting. Poonum wrote her first book, *Sincerely, Life: A Conversation to Find Yourself*, as a way to explore the depths of her personal philosophy on all life has to offer. Poonum writes pieces on culture, fitness, finance, and economics in her spare time, which can be found on her website. When Poonum is not working or writing, she can always be found at a concert or the gym, as music and fitness are two of her passions. Poonum currently resides in Dallas, Texas.

Connect with the Author

poonumdesai.com

Leave a Review

Will you please consider leaving a review for *Sincerely, Life: A Conversation to Find Yourself* on your platform of choice? Thanks to reviews, self-published authors can reach more readers like you.

Made in the USA
Coppell, TX
09 November 2020